Mysteries of the Forbidden Emerald Tablets

Billy Carson

MYSTERIES OF THE FORBIDDEN EMERALD TABLETS OF THOTH

BILLY CARSON

Copyright © 2025 by Billy Carson

All rights reserved.

This book or any portion thereof may not be reproduced or used in any manner whatsoever without express written permission from the publisher except for the use of brief quotations in critical articles, reviews, and pages where permission is specifically granted by the publisher.

Although the author and publisher have made every effort to ensure that the information in this book is correct, the author and publisher do not assume and hereby disclaim any liability to any party for any loss, damage, or disruption caused by errors or omissions, whether such errors or omissions result from negligence, accident, or any other cause. Likewise, the author and publisher assume no responsibility for any false information. No liability is assumed for damages that may result from the reading or use of information contained within. Read at your own risk. The views of this publication do not necessarily reflect the views of 4biddenknowledge.

ISBN 979-8-9925752-0-0

Books may be purchased by contacting the publisher and author at:

4biddenknowledge Inc.

2645 Executive Park Dr, Suite 419

Weston, FL 33331

http://4BK.TV

4biddenknowledge.com

Info@4biddenknowledge.com

Interior formatting by Winterwolf Press

Cover art created by Winterwolf Press

Cover art © 2024 by Billy Carson

About the Author

Billy Carson, Founder and CEO

Billy Carson is the founder and CEO of 4BiddenKnowledge Inc. and a 4X Best-Selling Author of *The Compendium Of The Emerald Tablets*, *Woke Doesn't Mean Broke*, *The Epic of Humanity*, and *Fractal Holographic Universe*. Additionally, he won the 2022 Stellar Citizens Award.

Mr. Carson is also the founder and CEO of 4BiddenKnowledge TV, a conscious streaming TV network, and the host of *Anunnaki: Ancient Secrets Revealed*, a new TV series that explores the ancient past from a fresh perspective with incredible insights into the development of an ancient global civilization.

Mr. Carson hosts the *4biddenknowledge Podcast* and is the Co-Host of the *Bio-Hack Your Best Life Podcast*. He is also a writer and contributor to Rolling Stone and Entrepreneur magazines, and Bizjournals.com.

Mr. Carson appreciates the dedication and hard work it takes to accomplish great things. He has earned a Certificate of Science (with an emphasis on Neuroscience and Artificial Intelligence) at MIT and a certificate in Ancient Civilization from Harvard University. Among his most notable achievements, Billy is the CEO of First-Class Space Agency, based in Fort Lauderdale, FL. His space agency is involved in researching and developing alternative propulsion systems and zero-point energy devices.

Works by 4biddenknowledge

Check Out Other Books by Billy Carson

Listen to the Music by Billy Carson

Introduction

The Emerald Tablets are ancient works by Thoth, the Atlantean Priest King. You can see him depicted below.

Depiction of Thoth

Thoth is traditionally portrayed with the head of an Ibis bird, yet he is not a bird-man. He is not a human being's body with a bird's head. His Ibis mask is a metaphor.

INTRODUCTION

The Ibis Bird

The Ibis Mask Metaphor

What's the ibis mask metaphor about?

Bringing darkness to light!

To understand this metaphor, you need to understand the Ibis bird. These birds spend hours repeatedly putting their long beaks deep into the mud, searching for sustenance beneath the surface.

It's like, man, do they even come up for air?

The birds search below the sod and the grass. They search the darkest places and bring what was hidden to light. That's why the head of the Ibis bird with its long beak symbolizes Thoth. Thoth's teachings probe the darker, unseen realms to reveal hidden truths; this symbolic connection emphasizes Thoth's mission to enlighten humanity, helping us move from obscurity toward the light of understanding.

Introduction

When you learn the history of Thoth, the Atlantean, you discover that he's traveled worldwide. He helped to rebuild and revive civilizations, and he kick-started brand-new civilizations. His sole purpose was to help bring humankind from darkness to light.

From Darkness to Light

Thoth tells us,

> "Know, O man, that light is thine heritage."

This statement reminds us that enlightenment is a pursuit and our inherent right. Light *is* our heritage. It's our birthright to be the light, see the light, and live in the light, including light from higher dimensions.

Thoth even talks about manifesting solid stone from light waves and cymatic frequencies of sound.

It sounds like science fiction, right?

You wouldn't be alone in thinking so. Many people dismissed these concepts as fantasy until a few years ago when scientists in a laboratory created solid matter from photons and sound.

That's right!

We have now created (or rediscovered) the scientific technology that Thoth talked about thirty-eight thousand years ago in the Emerald Tablets, and we continue to rediscover what has already existed from times long past. As the saying goes, "There are no new ideas." We only tap into "the Field" and download information that we feel is new but is actually ancient.

That's why I love my book, *Compendium of the Emerald Tablets*! In that book, I bridge ancient wisdom with modern insights, illustrating that the ancients knew and used the principles of what we now call quantum physics. Today, we are using ancient quantum physics. People already knew this stuff; it already existed and was taught, and adept initiates from all over learned this information.

Speaking of adept initiates, every single one of you reading this book is now an adept initiate in the ancient mysteries. You distinguish yourself from the masses by exploring these ancient teachings. You have gone the extra mile in your pursuit of knowledge.

And so, I applaud you!

What it Takes to Become an Initiate

It takes courage to walk this path. It takes courage to say, "This is what I will do. I'm going to sacrifice time with the family. I'm going to sacrifice time with the kids. I'm going to sacrifice time hanging out and having fun." Instead of going to a movie, the park, the beach, or wherever you could be, you stopped and said, "Hey, I'm going to spend this time gaining sacred and secret knowledge." And you're serious enough that you've invested time and money so that you can be here, at this moment, learning.

So, I applaud you because, based on how many people exist, very few are reading this book. Sure, I know that at least two hundred thousand or three hundred thousand people have heard me talk about these topics, yet most do not invest in themselves to do something about it, like buying and reading this book.

So, what does that tell you?

It tells you that you're one of the few awakeners, and you're on the quest for knowledge! Your commitment places you among a select group engaging with these teachings today.

We're in the age of awakening and the age of knowledge. However, the highest levels of knowledge will still only be available to the few

INTRODUCTION

who are on the knowledge quest–those on the hero's journey towards knowledge–people like you!

Your Companions on the Path to Knowledge and Enlightenment

The Emerald Tablets have passed through countless hands over the eons. Many people, including famous ones, touched, deciphered, and were inspired by these tablets. Sir. Francis Bacon, Sir. Isaac Newton, the Queen of Shiba, and Michael Dorell are just a few; the list goes on and on. I find it incredible how this work has inspired these critically acclaimed individuals and influenced entire religious movements. Despite their ancient origins, the teachings remain dynamic, continually inspiring new generations to seek hidden wisdom. Today, as we explore these texts together, we learn and contribute to the living tradition of these ancient teachings.

When I first learned about the Emerald Tablets, I started reading and they blew my mind! The more I dug into them, the more I saw, and the more enlightenment I gained.

Even in *Compendium of the Emerald Tablets*, you'll notice that Tablets 14 and 15 aren't broken down much because I wasn't ready to break them down at the time.

So, I decided to release the information in this book.

Therefore, let's assemble. Let's combine our energetic forces regardless of distance, time, or space. Let's link up. Let's quantum entangle with the thought waves and teach this knowledge to each other. Because, at the same time that I'm teaching, I'm also learning.

Now, let's dive in!

One
Location of the Emerald Tablets

The Emerald tablets

There are about five miles of Vatican archives, maybe even more extensive than that, underneath the Vatican in Rome. The Emerald Tablets have moved several times throughout history but are now located inside the Vatican archives, along with most of the books that "burned" at the Library of Alexandria.

The Library of Alexandria was a book heist. It was thievery–the most significant theft of knowledge in the known universe. It's still a mystery how the entire library seemed to have completely burnt down. I've been there and could envision how the theft happened. While fires were burning, books were being stolen, and I'm talking about a massive number of books.

The Alexandria Library

So, now you know that the books of Alexandria are at the Vatican, along with the Emerald Tablets. Well, all except for one tablet–The Emerald Tablet of Hermes.

Only one tablet, the Emerald Tablet of Hermes, resides outside the Vatican, proudly displayed at Cambridge University. You can actually go to Cambridge in the UK and see it with your own eyes. The rest of the tablets are in the Vatican.

Tablets 14 and 15

Now it's time to examine the last two remarkable tablets–Tablets 14 and 15. They were extremely important. They were exceptionally powerful, and you'll find out why very soon.

As we look closer at Tablets 14 and 15, we uncover teachings about Stargates, other dimensions, and astral travel—topics that remain as mysterious as they are captivating.

So, buckle up and put on your space suits! This is going to be powerful stuff.

Tablet 14 says,

> "List ye, O Man, to the deep hidden wisdom, lost to the world since the time of the Dwellers."

If you've read the Emerald Tablets of Thoth, you'll undoubtedly recall the concept of the "dwellers." These beings, referred to as gods with a lowercase 'g,' are distinct from what we traditionally think of as the uppercase 'God,' the omnipotent creator of the universe. While not omnipotent, these dwellers were revered as gods by the Atlanteans due to their advanced abilities and knowledge.

The Atlanteans recognized a clear distinction between the supreme God, the creator of all, and these powerful beings. The dwellers achieved a high level of consciousness and possessed remarkable abilities derived from their deep understanding of sensory perception and advanced technologies. This understanding allowed the

Atlanteans to honor these beings appropriately without confusing their abilities with the omnipotence attributed to the creator God.

The Dweller of Unal and How He Connects to Thoth and Sumerian Lore

In the first tablet, we meet the Dweller of Unal, who's revealed to be Thoth's father, E-R Enki. Enki might already be a familiar name if you've explored the Sumerian Tablets. Yes, that's right—Thoth's father and Enki from Sumerian lore are the same person. This connection ties Thoth's Atlantean background directly to those ancient Sumerian stories.

Enki's wisdom, once widely recognized and revered, has faded into the background through the ages. But today, as you immerse yourself in these texts, it's as if you're part of reviving a long-lost tradition. By linking past insights with present curiosity, you're not just learning history but actively engaging with knowledge that bridges centuries.

Are you ready for an exciting, blow-your-mind, reveal?

Earth is a portal!

The first key reveals that Earth itself is a portal:

> "Know ye this Earth is but a portal."

Earth is a portal that allows people to move from one physical location on the x, y, z axis to another on the x, y, z axis, anywhere within the known universe, not just on Earth itself.

Two
Portals of Mystery

Evidence that Earth is a Portal

According to scans, underwater pyramids are inside the Bermuda Triangle, right off the coast of Florida. Evidence of ancient Atlantis!

Bermuda Triangle

Also, if you could draw a line straight through the center from above, going down straight down into the ocean, straight through the center of the Bermuda Triangle, straight through the earth, straight to the other side, where do you end up on the other side of the planet?

You end up at the Yonaguni Pyramid and the Dragon's Triangle. You can even go for a dive and explore the underwater pyramid.

Underwater Pyramid

LIKE THE BERMUDA TRIANGLE, many crazy things happen in this area, such as the disappearance of boats, airplanes, and other things.

Why can you draw a line straight from the Bermuda Triangle to the other side of the planet and end at the Dragon's Triangle?

It's no coincidence! A portal connects these two locations. There have been many disturbances and disappearances in both places because the portal technology is malfunctioning; it's partly broken but still emits very exotic energy. Under specific conditions, specific times, and alignments, the portal activates. That's when people in boats, ships, airplanes, and everything else within the vicinity disappear.

Where did the ships, planes, and people go?

It's not exactly clear. Sometimes, the boat or the ship reappears, but usually, when it reappears, there's no crew.

In 2015, a tanker coming out of the UK (I believe it was from one of the Slavic countries) bringing supplies to the US took a shortcut through the Bermuda Triangle.

This is recent. You can Google this incident.

Advanced technologies were used to track the tanker, such as GPS tracking, sonar radar, and all the other things that work on this state-of-the-art ship.

Guess what happened to it.

A ship on the bottom of the ocean

IT DISAPPEARED in the Bermuda Triangle, but later, it appeared at the bottom of the Atlantic Ocean, sitting straight up and down with no damage.

But guess what?

No crew!

So, we're talking about a portal that exists—a still active portal. It's acting strangely, which clearly shows there's something wrong with it. Plus, it's super ancient.

Why is there something wrong with it?

No one knows. But we can guess. Perhaps tectonic plates have shifted in ways that could have broken the technology, causing it to act out of sorts.

MODERN PROOF **That Portals Exist On Earth**

NASA released a statement several years ago about discovering X points around the Earth. What are X points? X points are diffusion regions where portals naturally occur daily around planet Earth. Every single day, these X points appear.

Isn't that interesting?

X points appear consistently around the planet Earth!

The portals on Earth create direct paths to the sun, the moon, and even to other planets in the solar system. Researchers don't know where some go, so they've begun investigating how to activate and keep the portals open. They want to learn how to use the portals to travel from one place to another; that's peer-reviewed, actual science, and a public statement made by NASA, the space agency.

So, we've been speaking about the knowledge we've acquired from ancient times, which is now verifiable by modern science. Now, let's talk about something fascinating: Portal Guardians.

Thoth tells us that these portals aren't just mysterious passages; they are guarded by forces beyond human comprehension, referred to not as people but as powers. What exactly are these powers? Later, we'll explore that mystery, but we must first take a detour.

Before we go further, let's take a moment to consider some fascinating aspects of ancient Egyptian technology. I want to highlight the significance of the ankh and the djed—specifically, the djed, which resembles a Tesla coil. You can see depictions of the djed in various hieroglyphs across Egypt, often with an electric cable protruding from it. These images aren't just symbolic; they show the djed connected to devices like an electroplating apparatus and even what appears to be light bulbs in the Temple of Dendera.

Ankh and Djed

This isn't speculation. The existence of wireless energy transmission and the use of electricity by the ancient Egyptians is now recognized.

Ancient Egyptian Light Bulb

Mainstream historians and archaeologists can no longer deny this, especially given the millions of pieces of electroplated gold that have been found, dating back to ancient times. The ancient Egyptians harnessed electricity.

However, what is intriguing about this capacitor, the djed, is that it generated a technological phenomenon when you linked it with the ankh in a specific manner. That said, keep in mind that the ankh they used is not just a regular old everyday ankh-like jewelry but a specific type of ankh.

This specialized ankh with the djed inserted into its center was set to the resonant frequency of the atoms in the owner's body. In other words, combining the ankh and djed created some form of technology that resonated with the specific owner's atomic frequency.

Therefore, not everyone used the portals.

What's the catch?

Only an elite group of people had access to this technology. The owner had to be a dweller, a lord, a god, or a wisdom keeper–someone with extremely high-level access. This elite group had above top-secret clearance.

But wait...there's more!

Here's the key; the specific person's atomic frequency also had to be programmed into the Stargate or the portal. So, the portal knew! It was like, "Okay, I have twenty-five frequencies stored here, and if somebody tries to walk through here without one of these frequencies, I will obliterate them!"

The other less dramatic option was that the portal just wouldn't open for them, depending on its location and type of portal. Yes, they had various kinds of portals.

Amazing! Right? Now back to the portal guardians.

So, remember when I told you forces were guarding the portals? The Guardians are these frequencies!

Frequencies have power!

They have power over space-time, they have power over matter, and they even help create matter.

How Do We Know Frequencies Have Power?

Cymatics! Remember?

It's all connected!

As if that's not incredible enough, what if I told you there were the "Elite of the Elites?"

Lil was one of these people! He built something called a Doron Key.

- Key = Earth
- Doron = bond to heaven.
- (A Key that Bonded Earth to Heaven)

Bond, heaven earth, is the actual arrangement of words, but the meaning is clear.

This key allowed Lil to walk from his home world to Earth and back again.

So, these ancient gods had the ability and the knowledge to access these portals. They understood the frequency needed to activate the portals. Once activated, the gods could walk through them.

From the details shared in the Sumerian Tablets, it's clear that not all ancients had access to the advanced portal technology. Groups like the Ijiji, for instance, lacked the high-level clearance needed to use these portals. When their home planet neared our sun—a period known as a Shar—they relied on conventional space travel. Using the moon or Mars as way stations, they planned their journeys to rendezvous with their planet at the closest approach.

But remember, a select few could bypass these conventional routes entirely. These privileged beings used portals to walk directly from Earth to their home planet and back, and they kept their secrets closely guarded.

Keeping Portal Technology a Closely Guarded Secret

A Guardian at a portal

Why did the gods keep the portal technology a secret?

It's simple: they didn't want people to know how to access these portals and visit their homes!

Let's reread the quote to see how it all fits together.

> "List ye, O Man, to the deep hidden wisdom, lost to the world since the time of the Dwellers, lost and forgotten by men of this age. Know ye this Earth is but a portal, guarded by powers unknown to man."

Now that we know the guardians are frequencies, let's take a closer look at where these portals connect to that are not on Earth.

> "Yet, the Dark Lords hide the entrance that leads to the Heaven-borne land."

This passage appears to speak about another dimension—a location they're calling the Heaven-born land. Apparently, there are people born not on Earth but somewhere up in space—in the sky, in another location, or maybe even in another dimension. We can't know where the portal leads.

All we can really know is that the Heaven-born land is not Earth.

What's fascinating about this history is that all the major religions say their gods are not from Earth. They all descend from Heaven to Earth. Even the ancient Egyptian records talk about the time of Zep Tepi when the neptiru fell from heaven to earth and turned mud into a kingdom.

How coincidental is it that all these people are saying the same thing?

They're saying that people are being born elsewhere before arriving here. And the Emerald Tablets is talking about it specifically right here.

But wait. That's not all.

Reread this part of the text and tell me there's not something interesting.

> ". . . guarded by powers unknown to man. Yet the Dark Lords hide the entrance that leads to the Heaven-born land."

Let's go back again. . .

I'm sorry. . .

The dark lords?

What?!?

Three
Beings of Darkness and Light

The Dark Lords

These dark lords are who Thoth also calls "the Dark Brothers." These are the people ruling from behind the scenes. They are responsible for hiding all the amazing, powerful knowledge and technologies. Today, our dark lords are people who make up the Vatican, the governments of the world, the military-industrial complex, the people that run these three letter agencies, CIA, FBI, and so forth, and so on. All these people operate with no congressional oversight.

They get contracts from the Pentagon and so forth. They conceal and guard the secret knowledge they don't want the world to know about or have access to. Those are the dark lords–the people who create all the wars and fund the wars on both sides globally. These are the same dark lords Thoth talks about when he says,

"Yet the Dark Lords hide the entrance."

They're keeping the knowledge and technologies hidden from us. They're keeping us dumb and ignorant. They've trapped us in a mindset of thinking that anything futuristic or fantastical has to be some kind of sci-fi because it can't be real life. In reality, what you see in these sci-fi movies is closer to reality than the mundane life we've been living.

Thoth says,

> "That leads to the Heaven-born land. Know ye, the way to the sphere of Arulu."

Now, we're talking about something unique here. Thoth says it's guarded by barriers open only to the light-born man.

> "Upon Earth, I am the holder of the keys to the gates of the Sacred Land. Command I, by the powers beyond me, to leave the keys to the world of man."

This is why you're here today.

Let's break this down a little bit. The dark lords are hiding the entrance that leads to the Heaven-born land. We know the dark lords, but Thoth says,

> "Know ye, the way to the sphere of Arulu."

A sphere.

Well, we know that Earth is a sphere.

How do we know?

Besides our science, fundamental physics, and understanding, Thoth and many other ancient tablets, including Sumerian Tablets, talk about the earth being a sphere. It's spoken of in the Book of

Enoch and many other texts that you can find from all around the world.

But what's interesting about this passage is that Thoth refers to another sphere named Arulu. Arulu is a sphere that these portals apparently are linked to, and it's guarded by barriers opened only to the light-born man.

THE LIGHT-BORN MAN

Light-born

The light-born man is a man who has been born again, into the light.

We're born into darkness, but our mission and birthright are to seek the light and be born into the light. Being born again has nothing to do with getting doused in water, getting dunked in the lake, having some guy smash you into a pool, someone throwing you underneath the wave of the ocean, or someone taking your brand-new babies and splashing water on them. That's just the indoctrination of dogma, which means absolutely nothing. These rituals do nothing for the person, nothing for their spirit. Zero.

Being born again is all about understanding and learning, becoming an adept, being initiated in sacred and secret knowledge, accessing it, learning it, having a quench for it, discerning it, putting action behind it, utilizing it in your life, and teaching it.

When you can look back on your life, you should be able to see how far you've come. I can look back to even just two years ago and see where I was versus where I am now. I've been born again. We will all continue to be born again, over, and over, throughout this lifetime.

If you ever stop raising yourself to the next level, consciously and spiritually, then you're dying. And so, we're talking about being born into the light.

Did you see that Thoth says,

> "Upon Earth?"

This tells us that he's on Earth, and when he's on Earth.

> "I am the holder of the keys to the gates of the Sacred Land."

Thoth has the keys to the gates that give access to Arulu. He has the keys *and* the frequencies that provide access to the gates of the sacred land.

He says,

> "Command I, by the powers beyond me to leave the keys to the world of man."

What does this mean?

It means he left the keys and the frequencies to access the gates to us! And there are several ways to access them.

The keys have been left to us. We can access them if we so choose, if we are deemed worthy enough, and if we can tap into the correct frequencies to get past the powers that be.

We've arrived at the moment we've been waiting for, the time prophesied to us. The keys to the gates of Arulu were meant to be left on Earth for us to find at this very time. Profound knowledge and information were sent out tens of thousands of years ago through a ripple in spacetime.

And guess what?

We have now intersected with that wave right here, in our time. We are colliding with this ancient wave of knowledge and wisdom.

So, the mission set out from the past has traveled into our future, and here we are, meeting it head-on at this exact moment. We're blessed, indeed. It's an incredible time to be alive, to witness and be part of this unfolding!

As Thoth prepares to leave, he imparts a crucial lesson:

> "Before I depart, I give ye the Secrets of how ye may rise from the bondage of darkness."

This powerful statement sets the stage for transformation, indicating that freeing ourselves from our limitations is essential to achieving a state of enlightened existence. To access the gates and ascend, we must first become what he calls a light-born man.

Thoth explicitly instructs,

> "Cast off the fetters of flesh that have bound ye."

This metaphor urges us to let go of the earthly burdens we carry—be it material attachments, emotional ties, or deep-seated traumas that hold us back. Thoth reminds us that in this third-dimensional world, we often trap ourselves, playing the dual roles of prisoners and prison guards in our lives.

He emphasizes the necessity of liberation, saying,

"Rise from the darkness into the Light."

This ascent requires us to shed the weights that tether us to lower states of being. If you feel burdened by trauma, self-pity, or the consequences of past actions, you must recognize your own role in facing these challenges on the path to enlightenment.

Thoth's wisdom is clear: by recognizing that you have the power to change your circumstances, you empower yourself to rise into a higher state of consciousness.

What's the next step?

You love yourself wholeheartedly and completely!

That's right.

You feel the warmth of your love, your heart, loving yourself, loving your spiritual self, your higher self, loving every part of you.

Then it's time to forgive yourself. Look in the mirror and say, "I forgive you. I forgive you." While you say this, look directly into your own eyes.

"I forgive you."

That's right, you have the power to forgive yourself. Forgiveness is the key to releasing the fetters that bind. If you do just this one thing alone, forgive yourself, you will find freedom.

Tell yourself that you forgive yourself, and then look back at the mistakes that were made and write down, "How can I learn from these mistakes? How can I avoid this situation again? How can I prevent these things from happening again?"

Whatever it is that you condemn yourself for, whatever guilt you carry, let it go. When you completely love and forgive yourself, you have freed yourself to be born again. That's the real message the Bible was trying to convey before it got remixed.

Thoth says,

> "Rise from the darkness into the Light. Know ye, the soul must be cleansed of its darkness."

Cleansing the Soul of its Darkness

How do you cleanse your soul?

You must forgive yourself. You need to acknowledge your mistakes. Admit that you were wrong and recognize that you put yourself in this situation. You must take ownership and 100% responsibility for your life.

> "Know ye, the soul must be clean of its darkness. Ere ye may enter the portals of Light."

Once you're cleansed from your darkness, you then have the right to enter the portals of light.

> "Thus, I established among ye the Mysteries so that the Secrets may always be found."

Thoth left the breadcrumbs for us, and I'm giving you these breadcrumbs as we go deeper.

> "Aye, though man may fail into darkness, always the Light will shine as a guide."

So, what he's saying here is that there's a rise and fall of good and evil. There's a rise and fall of our own selves striving to seek the light. At times, we will move in realms of brightness, but at times, we'll also fall into the darkness; it is known that this can happen. In religion, they call it backsliding, but he's saying,

> "Though man may fall into darkness, always the Light will shine as a guide."

There's always going to be a beacon of light for you to look at. There's always going to be a lighthouse right on the shoreline for you to follow.

Light

For example, this book and *Compendium of the Emerald Tablets* serve as beacons of light to help get you back on track, to help bring you ashore safely.

> "Thus, I established among you the Mystery so that the Secrets will always be found. Aye, though man may fall into darkness, always, the Light will shine as a guide. Hidden in darkness, veiled in symbols, always the way to the portal will be found."

This means you will always find a way to the portal. Sure, it may be hidden in darkness and veiled in symbols. The way to the portal is ambiguous, it's hard to find, it's being covered up, it's being oppressed and suppressed. But the symbols themselves will lead you.

The symbols themselves!

> "Veiled in symbols, always the way to the portal will be found. Man in the future will deny the mysteries but always the way the seeker will find."

You see, he's talking about the seekers that are reading this book, right now. He's talking about you! He's saying specifically that the masses will shun this information, will scoff at it, will disbelieve it. But he's saying again that the truth seekers, the knowledge and wisdom seekers are going to be the ones that will always find this.

And that is us! We are the future seekers that he's referencing right now!

> "The way to the portal will be found. Man in the future will deny the mysteries but always the way the seeker will find. Now I command ye to maintain my secrets, giving only to those who ye have tested."

See, I tested you to be here and read this book. I literally tested you to be here. I didn't just say, I'm going to go on Instagram live to drop this knowledge. I was commanded not to freely give this information, until I test the receiver of the knowledge. What was the test? You bought this book. Not that it's going to make me rich. . . I'm going to donate most of the proceeds to kids that need help. But at the end of the day, it's a financial test. It's a financial sacrifice that you had to make–an energy sacrifice, making you to become worthy of being an initiate into this knowledge. That's the test. If this wasn't the twenty-first century, the test would've been something different. In this current era, this is the most likely way of testing someone to see if they are able and willing to be able to handle and take on this knowledge.

> "Now I command ye to maintain my secrets, giving only to those who ye have tested, so that the pure may not be corrupted, so that the power of Truth may prevail."

That's why you were tested to be reading this today. And the others that are not reading this, they failed the test. They heard the call, they felt the fire burning inside of them, but they didn't heed the call. You did!

> "List ye now to the unveiling of Mystery. List to the symbols of Mystery I give. Make of it a religion, for only thus will its essence remain."

So now, we're talking about the creation of religions and why they are all extremely similar to the Emerald Tablets. I've had a significant epiphany, one that has now been confirmed three times over, about the true identity of Thoth the Atlantean and who he might be recognized as in modern times.

Thoth instructed his most advanced initiates with a crucial task:

> "List ye now to the unveiling of Mystery. List to the symbols of Mystery I give. Make of it a religion for only thus will its essence remain."

His command was clear: transform this esoteric knowledge into a religion to ensure its transmission across generations. Embedded within these new religious tenets would be the encoded secrets of higher-level mysteries, hidden from the many but accessible to a discerning few.

Four
Beyond Reality

The Dimensions

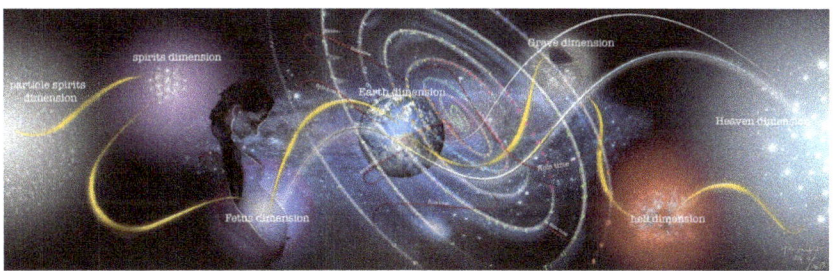

The Dimensions

"Regions there are two between–this life and the Great One."

In this verse, Thoth is talking about two locations–this life in the third dimension and the other life that exists outside of the third dimension.

He says,

"traveled by the Souls who depart from this Earth."

When your physical body ceases to function, marking the end of your earthly life, it does not signify the end of your existence. You are inherently eternal. When your physical body ceases to function and decomposes, releasing its atoms back into the system, your spirit is set free. Released from its corporeal confines, your spirit then transitions, moving from this three-dimensional existence to a higher realm, to your higher location.

The Matrix

"Traveled by the Souls who depart from this Earth. Duat, the home of the powers of illusion."

In this teaching, Thoth is speaking of the holographic matrix. Thoth tells us in earlier verses and in this one, that Duat is the secret access point of the holographic matrix itself. He also says Duat is the home of the powers of illusion. In other words, he's saying that this dimension is an illusion.

We're living in a testing ground, a proving ground. We're living in a program where illusion is embedded within us, around us, and throughout everything that exists in this third dimension.

It's all an illusion.

Think about this: there are eight billion people on Earth. Atoms are 99.9999% empty space. If I can remove all the empty space between the atoms in everyone's bodies, I can fit all eight billion people into one sugar cube.

We're not even here!

Our higher selves are transmitting to our lower selves, which are in this dimension. Here, we're given the illusion of solidity, the illusion of individuality, the illusion of separation, the illusion of distance. These are all illusions.

Thoth says,

> "Sekhet, Hetspet, the House of the Gods. Osiris, the symbol of the guard of the portal who turns back the souls of unworthy men."

Are you beginning to see where the Bible took its text from to create heaven and to create gates of heaven?

The gates of Arulu and Duat–those are the same as the gates of heaven that the Bible refers to.

Am I going to be allowed in? If not, am I going to "hell?"

The concepts of heaven and hell originated from this tablet. Osiris himself is the one who denies the souls of unworthy men.

Osiris

Osiris

Osiris is Orion–from Orion's belt

> "Beyond lies the sphere of the heaven-born powers. Arulu, the land where the Great Ones have passed. There, when my work amongst men has finished, will I join the Great Ones of my Ancient home."

Thoth is giving us a huge clue here!

After our bodies die, our spirit travels to Duat. Then it goes through Duat to Arulu, where the Great Ones reside. Yes, they are still alive and that's where they live. This is the place Thoth lives, and he claims to have the capability to choose when and where to incarnate. He can incarnate at will whenever and wherever he desires. He's also saying that this is a power all of us possess.

He says that when his work is done here, when his work among men has been finished,

> "Will I join the Great Ones of my Ancient home."

He's joining them at Arulu, the location where these Great Ones live.

> "Seven are the mansions of the house of the Mighty."

Interesting, right? Can you see the similarities with what the Bible says?

Jesus says,

> "In my father's house, there are many mansions. If there were not, I would not tell you so."

Here, Thoth says,

> "Seven are the mansions of the house of the Mighty."

I believe that Yeshua, A.K.A. Jesus, is actually another reincarnation of Thoth on this planet!

> "Seven are the mansions of the house of the Mighty; Three guards the portal of each house from the darkness."

So, each one of these seven houses is actually a portal leading to other places.

> "Three guards the portal of each house from the darkness."

The only way to access the houses is through the portal, and then from that portal you must go through the house to get to another location.

These aren't mansions made of blocks and stone, where you can walk into kitchens, bathrooms, and other living areas. The mansions referred to in the above verse are junction points between locations and dimensions–between the third dimension and other dimensions.

From this passage, we can also see that there are seven mansions–seven mighty locations owned and run by mighty people with guards at each portal–three guards at each location. So, there are twenty-one guards.

> "Fifteen the ways that lead to Duat."

There are fifteen ways that lead to Duat, that lead to this access point.

> "Twelve are the houses of the Lords of Illusion."

Now, here's where it gets very interesting and deep. We're getting ready to get into it now.

Those of you who can remember, I've talked a lot about dimensions. Along with Michi Okaku, many theoretical physicists believe that our universe consists of at least eleven dimensions. They reason that without eleven dimensions, our universe would collapse. Within those eleven dimensions, we exist in the third one.

Additionally, the peer-reviewed science from the Brain Institute demonstrates that the human mind is linked to eleven dimensions. In other words, our consciousness is at least eleven-dimensional.

Eleven or Twelve Dimensions

Artistic Representation of the Dimensions

Thoth isn't talking about only eleven dimensions. He's talking about twelve dimensions. There's one more dimension that the researchers have yet to discover or calculate for.

> "Seven are the mansions of the house of the Mighty. Three guards the portal of each house from the darkness. Fifteen the ways that lead to Duat."

There are fifteen access points to Duat, twelve are the houses of the Lord's Illusion. That means we're living in an illusion. We're living in a matrix.

The word, "illusion," is Thoth's way of speaking about the holographic matrix that exists–we're living inside of a created program, and there are twelve dimensions to this program.

> "Twelve are the houses of the Lords of Illusion, facing four ways, each of them different.'"

Thoth is saying that these dimensions are stacked and they also have access points–four ways each. These access points are Duats.

> "Forty and Two are the great powers."

That's forty-two.

> "judging the Dead who seek for the portal. Four are the Sons of Horace. Two are the Guards of the East and West of Isis, the mother who pleads for her children, Queen of the Moon reflecting the Sun."

In this passage, Thoth says,

> "Forty and Two are the great powers."

He's talking about frequencies again.

> "Judging the Dead who seek for the portal."

This passage means that if your spiritual energies don't match the frequencies that are on this energetic grid, your soul is not permitted to enter into Arulu. Your soul ends up somewhere else. He does not say it ends up hell; it just doesn't give you access to the Great Ones.

The Merkaba

Let's talk about the star tetrahedron of the Merkaba. The Mer Ka Ba.

Thoth says,

> "Ba is the essence, living forever. Ka is the Shadow that man knows as life. Ba cometh not until Ka is incarnate."

Let's break this down, the Mer Ka Ba:

- Mer refers to light
- Ka refers to the spirit
- Ba refers to the body

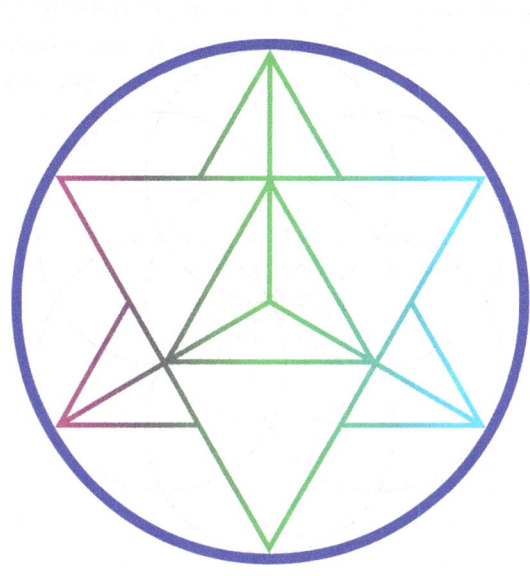

Merkaba

"Ba is the essence, living forever, Ka is the Shadow that man knows as life. Ba cometh not until Ka is incarnate. These are mysteries to preserve through the ages."

THOTH IS SAYING that Ba is the essence that lives forever. That means we're already eternal so we can stop fighting for eternity, stop begging for eternity, stop asking some other deity to come and give you eternal life, stop calling on the name of Jesus, because you're just saying, "Hail Zeus." You can stop begging Jesus to give you eternal life, begging him to forgive you for your sins. It's worthless.

We are all already eternal!

We are existing and have always existed and we will always exist. The holographic matrix has us completely subdued in this third density, leaving us blinded at this moment in time. The good news is that our incarnation in this matrix is temporal. We live in a testing ground or proving ground.

"The Ba cometh not until Ka is incarnate."

"The Ka is the Shadow of life."

Once the incarnation comes back, the Ba reconnects with the Ka. And you keep replaying this game repeatedly, to see how high you rank.

When I was a kid, I had an Atari 2600. It consisted of one joystick and one button. In Donkey Kong, you had to go through several levels. These games are just like life; you must jump over barrels and smash things at the right time. When you complete your tasks successfully, you gain points; you gain new lives, and your eternity becomes more assured as you do better and better.

But if you make a mistake and get rolled over by a barrel, what happens?

You die.

And when your body dies, well, now you reincarnate. So, you must use another player–another avatar. Another man pops up and you keep on playing the game. But this time, when you get to the level with the challenge that ended your previous game, you remember that barrel.

See?

You remember the challenges from previous lives, and now, you know how to jump over that hurdle. It doesn't kill you this time. And you go up a few more levels and then the game gets harder on every new level. And maybe you get killed again. Then you incarnate again.

You go through the first, second, third, and fourth levels with ease because you've conquered them many times before. Then the game gets extremely difficult again. The higher the level, the more difficult it gets. Upon each death, you must start from scratch and rebuild all over again. The ultimate goal is to get to the top level.

You see, the video games we've created are fractals of what exists throughout the entire universal matrix. We only recreate what's happening to us in a more rudimentary form.

The Keys of Life and Death

Keys

"Keys are they of life and Death. Hear ye now the mystery of mysteries: learn the circle beginningless and endless, the form of He

> who is One and in all. Listen and hear it, go forth and apply it, thus will ye travel the way that I go."

In this passage, Thoth speaks about preparing our spirit body to understand what it needs to do to be able to follow in his footsteps.

> "Keys are they of life and Death."

He's talking about keys, which Yeshua from the Bible also speaks about. I will write more about this shortly.

> "Hear ye now the mystery of mysteries: learn the circle beginningless and endless,"

I believe in this passage he is referring to the cycle of life–the rise and fall of life that happens–this endless circle that happens of birth, growth, death, reincarnation, repeatedly.

> "the form of He who is One and in all. Listen and hear it, go forth and apply it."

Do you see that key word here is, "apply?"

Until you apply knowledge, it's worthless. It means nothing. Applied knowledge is power. Knowledge by itself is worthless. Knowledge has no power until you apply the knowledge. Then, it has actual power.

> "Thus will ye travel the way that I go."

Once action is applied, then you will begin to move.

> "Mystery in Mystery, yet clear to the Light-born. the Secret of all I now will reveal. I will declare a secret to the initiated, but let the door be wholly shut against the profane."

The only people reading this book are initiates. You've been initiated. The people that are not reading this book, who are just waiting for me to hop on a regular old YouTube video, the door's closed on them. See? I follow the commands.

> "Mystery in Mystery, yet clear to the Light-born."

It's clear to us.

> "the Secret of all I now will reveal. I will declare a secret to the initiated, but let the door be wholly shut against the profane. Three is the mystery, come from the great one. Hear, and Light on thee will dawn."

The sun will rise. When the sun rises, it's going to give you an illumination–you will be illuminated by this knowledge.

> "Three is the mystery, come from the great one. Hear and Light on thee will dawn. In the primeval, dwell three unities. Other than these, none can exist. These are the equilibrium, source of creation: one God, one Truth, and one point of freedom."

There's three primeval entities that dwell in this particular realm.

Looking through the Emerald Tablets and various texts on Thoth the Atlantean, it's clear he goes by many names. We have Dehuti, Djehuti, Ku Ku Kan, Lord Pecal, Verakocha, and even Thoth the Mabi down in Australia. You might also recognize him as Mercury, Odin, or Thor across different cultures.

Thoth | Hermes Trismegistus | MERCURY.

Incarnations of Thoth

YET WITH ALL THESE titles and legendary status, there's one thing he consistently does not do: he never claims to be God. He doesn't present himself as the creator of the universe. It's fascinating—no matter where you find him or what name he's using, his role remains that of a guide or teacher, not a divine creator.

As a matter of fact, there was a time when people groveled at his feet and he said, "Hey, no, no, no, don't do that. I'm a son of Atlantis."

Sometimes, Thoth calls himself the "son of man." Now, think about that—because Yeshua, frequently mentioned in the Bible, also called himself the son of man. Pretty striking resemblance, don't you think? Today, I'm laying out the case that Yeshua is actually Thoth the Atlantean. Yep, the same guy, just wearing a different hat in another era.

This story, it's been twisted and retold so many times, but when you strip it all back, I'm convinced they're one and the same. Just another version, another life of this eternal figure. We're really talking about the same person across histories.

When Thoth speaks of One God, he's talking about monotheism.

"one God, one Truth, one point of freedom."

Here's where Thoth lays it out plain and simple: there is a God, but it's not him. It's not Enki, Nlil, Anu, Amenrah, or any of the big names we usually hear about. And it's definitely not any of the goddesses like Ishtar, Isis, or Inhersag either. This is the first time he's spelled it out so clearly—none of them are the ultimate God.

Five
The Universal Balance

The Trinity

A symbolic representation of the Trinity

Thoth says that there's

> "one God, one Truth, one point of freedom. Three come forth from the three of balance:"

In this passage Thoth is speaking about the Trinity.

You are now being revealed the actual true Holy Trinity.

> "all life, all good, all power. Three are the qualities of God in his Light-home: Infinite power, Infinite Wisdom, Infinite Love. Three are the powers given to the Masters: To transmute evil, assist good, use discrimination. There are three things inevitable for God to perform: Manifest power, wisdom, and love."

Let's go through this passage and let's break it down even deeper.

> "Three is the mystery, come from the great one."

Who's the great one?

The great one is God.

THE BIBLE DOES NOT SPEAK of the Same God that Thoth Speaks of.

I have always said that I believe that there is a God. I just don't believe that the one written in that biblical text is the creator of the universe. That's a person. As a matter of fact, it's a very evil person.

Why do I make this claim?

Because, when you add up all the deaths that were sanctioned by God in the Bible–all the murdering and killing–God kills over three million people, while the devil doesn't kill anyone!

So, who's doing all the killing in the Bible?

All of the killing in the Bible is attributed to God!

But this being has nothing to do with the creator of the universe.

> "Three is the mystery, come from the great one. Hear, and Light on thee will dawn. In the primeval, dwell three unities."

Thoth is speaking about the Trinity. These unities are the Trinity.

> "Other than these, none can exist."

In other words, Thoth is saying that without the Trinity, there's nothing here. Without this, these three things, nothing in the entire universe exists!

> "These are the equilibrium source of creation: one God, one Truth, one point of freedom."

He's talking about equilibrium. He's talking about a harmonic balance, a specific frequency that exists. That frequency is what is responsible for everything that exists in the entire known universe.

> "Three are the qualities of God in his Light-home: Infinite power, Infinite Wisdom, Infinite Love."

So, now you can distinguish between what the biblical says about God's qualities and what Thoth says about God's qualities. You can see that there's a huge difference!

Thoth says a quality of God is Infinite Wisdom.

Infinite Wisdom

Just off the top of my head, I can go to the Bible and tell you, the God of the Bible does not have infinite wisdom.

Do you want proof?

In the Bible, it's not uncommon for God to show up, scratch his head (*my dramatic effect added*), and ask questions that he apparently does not have the answer to.

For example, he questioned Adam. "Hey, how come Adam and Eve have clothes on now? How'd they get this knowledge? Who told him to do this?"

This clearly shows that the God of the Bible is not as smart as the God that Thoth Speaks of. The God of the Bible has no Infinite Wisdom.

Want another example?

God shows up at the Tower of Babel, when human beings had built this tower into the heavens, and he's shocked again.

"How in the world did they make this tower? Who taught them how to do this? How come they got the ability to do this?"

Does that sound like Infinite Wisdom to you?

So again, we're talking about two different Gods, two different entities. One is God according to Thoth and then there's another being who, while smarter than the average human, doesn't quite measure up to divine intelligence. This other being isn't a deity but merely a person with a bit more insight.

Infinite Power

The God Thoth speaks of has Infinite power.

The God of the Bible has no infinite power because the God of the Bible can't control its own creation, it can't control its own angels that it supposedly created. It can't control situations that are occurring. It can't control people becoming ruthless or riotous or evil. It has no power. It can't control anything. This God of the Bible's creations run around rampant and out of control, and he has no power over them. So obviously, and clearly, this God is not the God that Thoth is talking about.

Infinite Love

Clearly, if you go to the Bible, Infinite Love is very limited.

What kind of loving God goes around killing everybody?

Every time you turn around, he's killing people left and right. He's killing and murdering innocent women and children left and right.

Read the book of Deuteronomy. He's telling people to go and kill in his name. Kill the women, kill the children. He says, "You can even rape the virgins. Bring the spoils of war back to me."

Why would God need spoils of war? Again, proving that the God of the Bible is not the creator of the universe; that it's just a regular old guy that puts on his pants one leg at a time.

Thoth is talking about the real creator–infinite love, infinite wisdom, and infinite power.

He says, "Three are the powers given to the Masters: To transmute evil, assist good, use discrimination."

These are the three powers.

Transmute Evil

Now, we're talking about alchemy, which was taught in the land of Chem, at Al-chem-y, chemistry, right? So, we're talking about alchemy, where he is talking about transmuting evil. He's talking about taking darkness and bringing darkness to the light. If you look at it from a different level of the metaphor, look at all the ancient sages and wisdom keepers that have been written about in all these different texts, all throughout the ages, they always seem to hang out with the rough crowd. They always seem to draw attention from the rough crowds–illiterate people, drunkards, alcoholics, prostitutes. In the Bible, Jesus is hanging out with prostitutes, drunk people, criminals, ex-cons, right? Why? Because you must go into the darkness to deliver the light.

If I gather everyone reading this book into one big room and we share our knowledge back and forth, and we don't leave that room, eventually, we will get to a point where we all have roughly the same level of knowledge. Maybe a little here, a little up here, a little down here. But roughly on average, we'll average out to have about the same knowledge base. If we continue to stay in that room and not leave that room, how much good are we doing the universe?

Six
Illuminating the Shadows

How much good are we doing for mankind?

We've put ourselves on a pedestal. We've put ourselves on a throne. We've sat in a room together, and we've congregated for who knows, decades, eons, hundreds of years, whatever the number is, to share our knowledge with each other. That's becoming egotistical and evidence of hoarding knowledge, because the knowledge can't break past our own circle.

We're in the light. We made it to the light, but we're not bringing anything else to the light. So now, we're useless.

We're saying, "Oh, we got light now, but we're going to put a cap on top of this light. We're going to put this light in a box." Then we're no better than the dark lords. We're no better than the Dark Brothers, who are hoarding knowledge.

But if we leave that room after gaining that wisdom and that knowledge, and go into places where people are in darkness and begin to drop seeds of wisdom on them, we can then watch those seeds grow and we can even water those seeds from time to time and watch them grow from little tiny saplings into nice, strong trees with deep roots over time.

And that process is duplicatable. You see, that's what needs to be done. We can't hoard the knowledge—we have to test people to see how hungry they are, but at the same time, we have to find creative ways to go into the darkness and bring darkness to light. I do it all the time.

One of my techniques that I use is offering my lifestyle as a bait.

My Lifestyle

I have nice luxury things because I like to live the life of what I consider to be abundance. But I use those things as tools to reel in the younger generation, because I know the younger generation enjoys luxury. They like to see nice watches; they like to see nice cars. They like to see nice houses; they like to see nice vacations. They like to see nice clothes. So, I do those things. I go into darkness, utilizing my own bait, and I cast a reel out.

But I've got bait on the end of my hook. The bait is my lifestyle. It hooks them; it catches them. They're like, "Man, this guy, he doesn't look that old. He looks like he is forty or fifty years old. He's got nice stuff. He looks like he living a good life, and he is dropping this knowledge. I want to find out more about what this guy has to say."

I cast out my reel, and some people just don't see it. They just don't understand. "Oh, he's showing off and he's trying to show people what he's got."

I've been a millionaire for a long time–a multimillionaire.

No, what I'm doing is I'm going into the darkness. In this day and age, I am not going to walk into bars and strip clubs and the like because that is just not my style of operation or personality. I don't naturally do those things. Some people do, and that's great. They can utilize those areas to grab people and reel them in.

For me, the way I see it, using my lifestyle as bait works best for casting a wide net. Once I've got people's attention, that's when I can start reeling them in with the knowledge. Sure, some of the information might not stick, some might just pass through without a second thought, but some seeds of awareness will definitely spread, growing the tree of knowledge as it's shared among more people.

That's what it's all about–Understanding that, understanding how to transmute evil, and assisting good.

Assisting People that are Doing Good, Acting Good, Trying to be Good

The key to helping others is to be of service. Help when and where you can. It doesn't always have to be financial. I don't like people pulling on me, asking for loan every five seconds.

However, I go above and beyond to find ways to help through other channels, such as communities and schools. To support them, I match donations made during my live sessions, on my Instagram and TikTok reels, and in other ways. I also match the money raised through giveaways and raffles.

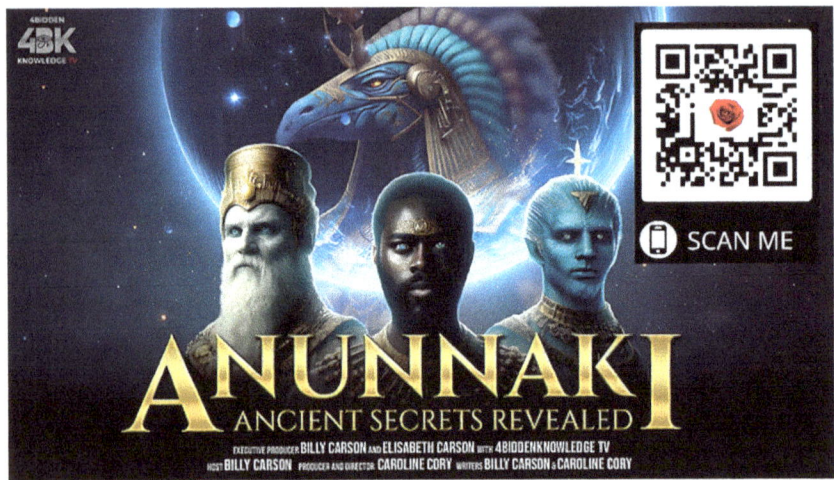

Anunnaki QR Code

4BiddenKnowledge TikTok

Mysteries of the Forbidden Emerald Tablets

. . .

4BiddenKnowledge Instagram

Compendium of the Emerald Tablets

4BiddenKnowledge.com

Coach Billy

Mysteries of the Forbidden Emerald Tablets

Billy Carson

I find creative ways to help people; to do good, and I use discrimination. This term doesn't mean discrimination as in segregation of blacks and whites and things like that. It's like using logic to figure out when and where you should be acting, helping, assisting, alchemizing or not. It means recognizing the people you can and cannot speak with.

WITHIN THE FIRST few sentences of speaking with a religious zealot, I already know whether I can get through to them or not. I use discrimination. I can't waste my life force. I walk away after dropping a seed, but I do it in a way that leaves an impact without being offensive.

You must give people a chance to find a way to grow. So, I drop seeds here and there, but I don't force anything on anybody, not even on my own kids. All of my kids believe in different things. I don't force anything on them. If they have questions, they know where to find me and they know I'll talk to them. Pretty powerful stuff.

Seven
Manifesting Divine Truth

Manifestations of Our True God Power

"Three are the things inevitable for God to perform:"

We are God walking in the flesh; we are a version of God. We are a fractal of God; and so, we have this capability as well.

The three things that are inevitable when we recognize our true God Power, are that we will:

- manifest power
- manifest wisdom
- manifest love

This is our birthright, because the same divine spark that created everything in *His* universe and gave out these commandments to be written, is the same divine spark that inhabits every individual atom in each of our bodies. And so, we are commanded to command ourselves, to manifest power, wisdom, and love, no matter where we go.

Walk in your true power. Understand your divine power. Believe in yourself. Have faith in yourself.

Operate in wisdom. Apply your knowledge.

And of course, manifest love. Love and abundance, everywhere with everyone.

Understanding that some people are not on the level you are consciously, but that doesn't give you the right to look at them side eyed, to laugh at them, to pick at them.

Treat them with dignity, respect and love.

Drop a seed and wait for that seed to grow. You may never see that person again, but that one seed you dropped out of empathy and love can change the timeline of the entire legacy of future generations.

That's how much power you can manifest.

The Divine Powers

> "Three are the powers creating all things: Divine Love possessed of perfect knowledge, Divine Wisdom knowing all possible means, Divine Power possessed by the joint will of Divine Love and Wisdom."

These are the three powers that are creating all things.

This divine spark, all this divine knowledge, it's literally inhabiting every atom in your body. Every nucleus is vibrating with this frequency. You just have to recognize it.

"Divine Love possessed of perfect knowledge, Divine Wisdom knowing all possible means, Divine Power possessed by the joint will of Divine Love and Wisdom."

"Three are the circles (states) of existence: The circle of Light where dwells nothing but God, and only God can transverse it;"

God exists in the circle of light that is outside of these dimensions. Only God can traverse it. You've heard me talk about this so many times. I repeated through my videos over the years that the God that created this entire universe is not in here with us.

We are the emanation of that God.

We ourselves, everything. Every atom in here; the atoms in my body, the atoms in the microphone, the atoms in the books, the atoms in the table, the atom in the chair. Every atom that exists in the entire universe is a version of God living subjectively, so that it may realize and understand what it's like to be in this dimension in everything in this universe.

But the creator itself is not in here. In other words, the source that has initiated this holographic matrix into existence with whatever programming code or divine code that it came up with, it can only be traversed by God itself. There's nobody else that can get to that dimension or that location, other than the creator itself.

"The circle of Chaos, where all things by nature arise from death."

What happens when you die?

They throw you in a box, if you're getting buried. Some people get buried right into the dirt, but it doesn't matter. Every atom in your body is recycled back into the system again. And out of your death, the death of your corporeal physical body, life comes back.

Life comes back!

THE CIRCLE of Life

Artistic Representation of the Circle of Life

It's a cycle. It's a circle, right?

> "The circle of Chaos where all things by nature arise from death; the circle of Awareness where all things spring from life. All things animate are of three states of existence:"

All things that invigorate you are animating this avatar body. Your brain opens portals into other dimensions to download your higher self; without it, your body would not be able to animate. You are downloading a stream of consciousness at a frequency that gives you your particular characteristics. And that light body, which is you, is animating this avatar. Once the avatar ceases to exist, it releases the light body, and the light body is then sent back to its higher self.

Well, it's not really sent back, it's always there. It's a beam that's being sent down into this lower density to animate. But the physical body then regenerates or rejuvenates through recycling until these atoms recycle into a format that can encapsulate a new frequency or an existing frequency that's out there, of spirit to be reanimated all over again.

That's why they call it a circle, or I like to call it a cycle.

It Always Comes in Threes

> "All things animate are of three states of existence: chaos or death, liberty and humanity and felicity of Heaven. Three necessities control all things, beginning in the Great Deep, the circle of chaos, and plenitude in Heaven. Three are the paths of the soul: Man, Liberty, and Light."

Let's start with the evolution of a sentient being:

You start as a man; then you must realize how we gain our liberty in order to get into the light. That means we need to figure out how to get free.

How can we get freedom?

Liberty is freedom.

Right now, there are eight billion people on this planet being controlled by fewer than a hundred individuals. Many of us believe we're free, but that's an illusion. In some countries, freedom, as we understand it in America, the UK, or Canada, simply doesn't exist. Some people are well aware that they aren't free. But in reality, all eight billion of us are prisoners. We're confined by invisible lines called borders that we can't cross without permission.

In some countries, like North Korea, people can't leave at all. Similarly, Egyptians find it tough to leave Egypt. Only a very small number of people—those who can afford to pay the right people—manage to get out, depending on factors like finances. For the vast majority, leaving isn't an option. Then there are places like Cambodia, where getting a visa to come to America, for example, is extremely difficult. There's a lot of restrictions, these invisible lines that have been created, keeping us locked, keeping us prisoners on our own planet.

Prison Planet

Along with the lack of access to the criminal justice and medical systems, there is the prison of taxation, employment, and educational systems. I could go on and on and on. All these institutions are merely variations of prisons and jails. And then there is the jail-jail, where actual people are imprisoned in most countries without any chance of real rehabilitation. There are perhaps two or three nations that genuinely prioritize rehabilitation. The rest of the world only seeks to profit from the mental illness of others by locking them up and hoping they never fully recover. This is an attempt to keep the individuals in the system and continue to make money off of them. They have capitalized prison.

We are living in that type of a situation where everything we hear, touch, feel, say, speak, is being controlled. I can't hop on YouTube and talk about certain things. I have to use code words, or they'll delete my account and cancel my paycheck. I'm a prisoner. I have no liberty in that area. And this is true for every living person who is not a member of the wealthy, powerful families who rule the show.

So, where do we go from here?

We, as a people, in order to get to the light, we have to begin to claim our freedom, our liberty, and it starts with claiming one liberty at a time. I'm now at the point where I've tapped into some of the light because I've claimed enough of my liberties.

We have to release ourselves from religious dogma, from political dogma, and from poli-tricks. We have to release ourselves from the systematic dogma of the news in the media, that is put out to trick, entice, distract. The elite's main focus is to generate fear so they can mold and shape you in the direction that they want you to go for their use and manipulation.

We must understand that the natural evolutionary process of man is not as a prisoner. Humanity rises, joins with one another, and recognizes that power is essentially found within the people.

Together, we cooperate, strategize, and assert our right to liberty on this earth. We take back command of our world.

The next natural progression on mass, is we reach the light. Some of us will make it through this process and see the light a little sooner, or at least some of it. There's even levels to the light.

But this is the evolutionary process; man, liberty, and light.

One of the biggest obstacles I've seen is the lack of effort to seek knowledge. This has been a huge hindrance, but I have to admit, it's slowly getting better. I've been at this for a very long time—you have no idea. But in this era, I can see progress. People are starting to make more of an effort to learn.

Eight
A Journey to Enlightenment

Hiding Behind the Bushes

Hiding behind A Bush

I remember hiding in the bushes of my old neighborhood, talking to people because I couldn't let anyone else hear our conversation. I could only speak to a couple of people—literally two. Looking back now, I realize that took a lot of courage. Over time, I've seen things evolve.

I'm talking about starting from the 1970s. From talking in the bushes, to the '80s on VHS tapes, then moving to cassette tapes in the late '80s. By the '90s, I was exchanging audio information on CDs, and then onto DVDs. Eventually, I transitioned to web forums. I think the original 4bidden Knowledge web forum is still online—it started back in 2010, or maybe 2008 or 2009, somewhere around then. From web forums, I moved to websites and blogs.

Now, I'm on TV, having been on over a thousand TV shows and well over five thousand podcasts. I even have my own TV network, dedicated to discussing these topics and this information. On top of that, I'm teaching private online workshops and classes to a global audience.

I remember in the early 1990s, reading about the prophecy of the Hopis. They predicted a time in the future when the world would be connected by a web—a worldwide web where information could travel instantaneously around the globe. When I read that, I knew deep down that if I could just stay alive long enough, my information would eventually reach everyone on this planet.

And I made it.

I remember watching TV and seeing this commercial. It was just a black screen with big, bold white letters: ibm.com. That was the entire commercial—no people, no taglines, nothing. This was in 1997, during an NBA basketball game on a Saturday afternoon. The commercial kept airing, over and over again.

I knew those commercials cost a lot of money. I couldn't help but wonder, what in the world does this mean? Why would anyone spend that kind of money on a commercial like this with no information?

TV Screen with IBM commercial

The next day, I went to the Barnes & Noble bookstore, and I asked the lady at the front desk, "Have you heard of this ibm.com? I'm trying to figure out what they're talking about. Do you happen to know?"

She said, "Oh, yes, that's the worldwide web. There's a whole section over there."

I went, "What? The worldwide web? I made it!"

I went to that section, and I realized, I'm living in the era of the information age.

I made it to the information age!

So you see, conversations behind the bushes gave way to VHS tape trades, information-containing cassette tapes and, eventually, the worldwide web. More people began to participate as a result of exchange and trade.

And so, this knowledge now has the possibility to propagate at an exponential rate around the entire planet, because of the age that we're living in. We made it to this time and this era where knowledge is to be shared around the entire planet, and that those who are seeking true wisdom and knowledge will have access to it in a way like never before. We're living in the beginning of the tetra yuga that literally is going to help usher mankind back towards the golden age.

When I hear people, including myself at times, getting down on humanity and thinking everything is just a wreck and a mess, I realize that's not entirely correct.

Progress Has Been Made

Even with the progress I've witnessed since 1977, there's been significant change. From our human perspective, it seems gradual because our lifespans have been shortened. If we lived the longer lifespans that were genetically intended for us, this timeframe would pass in the blink of an eye. The struggles and woes of humanity would appear to last only a short while. But with our shortened lifespans, everything feels prolonged and drawn out, creating an illusion that spiritually weighs us down. We struggle to make sense of it.

Let's put things in perspective by looking at the Earth. The planet is billions of years old. On a geological timescale, human beings have been here for less than a blink of an eye. If our existence were measured by the ticks of a clock, humans wouldn't even make one full tick in a single second. That's how brief our time has been on this world, in this third dimension. In geological terms, we've just arrived.

When you look at things from that perspective, you suddenly realize how far consciousness has come in just the last thirty years, and you are filled with hope, fervor, excitement, and optimism.

People say, *"How can you be so optimistic about humanity?"*

Well, I'm not viewing it from the perspective of someone who expects to live around 75-80 years, which is a limited view. From that standpoint, it seems like a lot of time has passed and things are still ongoing. But I'm looking at it on a geological timescale. From that vantage point, things are moving at a pretty rapid pace, and everything is actually right on schedule. In divine time, everything happens as it should, and we're exactly where we need to be.

By gaining this knowledge, traveling the world, meeting sages and wisdom keepers, learning this wisdom, and applying it, the mission is ultimately to help nudge mankind in the right direction, back towards a golden age where we belong. Nowhere is it written that we have to fall; instead, we should rise to that level and remain there continuously over time, rather than reach it and fall again.

Thoth says,

> "List ye, O man, to this mystery. Long in the past before ye were man-born,"

Before you were born as a man.

He's referring to the time before you were born into the flesh. In other words, this one part of the sentence is literally telling us that we existed before we were born as men. He is letting us know here that we existed before we were born as man.

"Long in the past, before ye were man-born, I dwelled in Ancient Atlantis. There in the Temple, I drank of the Wisdom poured as the fountain of Light from the Dweller."

The same fountain where waters run is referenced in the biblical text as well. The biblical text is from God while the Emerald Tablet is from the dweller–the dweller, who happens to be his father in this particular text. In the Bible, Yeshua, AKA Jesus references God as his father.

Nine
The Radiance of Creation

The Flower of Fire

Flower of fire

> "Give the key to ascend to the Presence of Light in the Great world."

Give the key to ascend–this is moving back towards a golden age.

> "To the Presence of Light in the Great world. Stood I before the Holy One enthroned in the flower of fire."

Thoth is talking about the energetic flower of life. He's saying that, and I've said this before–there's a post that I made years ago that went super viral—that the face of God is the flower of life.

Guess what? People were going crazy!

I am going to repeat this phrase: the face of God *is* the flower of life!

And once again, people scoffed. They were like, "Ah, what are you? Is he crazy?"

The face of God is the flower of life!

> "Veiled was he by the lightnings of the darkness, else my Soul by the Glory have been shattered."

Thoth is saying that this being that he's standing before is enthroned in the flower of fire.

The flower of fire is the flower of life.

*

The Flower of Life Symbol

He's also saying that it's so powerful and energetic that if he wasn't veiled—if he wasn't covered to block some of this energy—it would've shattered him.

> "Forth from the feet of his Throne like the diamond, rolled forth four rivers of flame from his footstool, rolled through the channels of clouds to the Man-world."

We are talking about an experience he had in a higher dimension, where he is now fleeing that higher level, entering the third dimension, and even having an impact on the world of humans.

> "Filled was the hall with Spirits of Heaven. Wonder of wonders was the Starry palace."

He is in an amazing place.

> "Above the sky, like a rainbow of Fire and Sunlight, were formed the spirits. Sang they the glories of the Holy One. Then from the midst of the Fire came a voice: "Behold the Glory of the first Cause." I beheld that Light, high above all darkness, reflected in my own being. I attained, as it were, to the God of all Gods, the Spirit-Sun, the Sovereign of the Sun spheres. Again came the Voice: "There is one, even the First, who hath no beginning,"

Do you see where the Bible gets a lot of his texts from now?

A lot of this has been copied almost word for word into the Bible.

Let's go back a little bit here.

> "Sang they the glories of the Holy One. Then from the midst of the Fire came a voice: "Behold the Glory of the first Cause."

That's eerily reminiscent to a verse in the New Testament, in the Book of Revelation, actually.

> "And whenever the living creatures give glory and honor, and thanks to him who is seated on the throne, who lives forever and ever, the twenty-four elders fall down before him who is seated on the throne and worship him, who lives forever and ever. They cast their crowns before the throne saying, 'Worthy are you, oh Lord God, to receive glory and honor and power, for you created all things. By your will, they existed

and were created. Holy, holy is the Lord God Almighty, who was and is and always is to come.' And the four living creatures, and each of them with six wings are full of eyes all around and within, and day and night, they never cease to say, 'Holy, holy, holy is the Lord God Almighty'."

A scene in Book of Revelations

This passage is from the Book of Revelation. And then, when I go back to where we were here, "

> Above the sky, like a rainbow of Fire and Sunlight, were formed the spirits. Sang they the glories of the Holy One."

They sang the glories. I just gave you the song that these people sang.

> "Then from the midst of the Fire came a voice: "Behold the Glory of the first Cause." I beheld that Light, high above all darkness, reflected in my own being. I attained, as it were, to the God of all Gods, the Spirit-Sun, the Sovereign of the Sun spheres. Again came the Voice: "There is one, even the First, who hath no beginning,"

Between those verses and phrases, is virtually the same thing; just written in two different ways.

> "Again came the Voice: "There is one, even the First, who hath no beginning, who hath no end; who hath made all things, who govern all, who is good, who is just, who illumines, who sustains." Then from the throne, there poured a great radiance, surrounding and lifting my soul by its power. Swiftly I moved through the spaces of Heaven, shown was I the mystery of mysteries, shown the Secret heart of the cosmos. Carried was I to the land of Arulu, stood before the Lords in their Houses."

He's at these gates now.

> "Opened they the Doorway so I might glimpse the primeval chaos."

Primeval Chaos.

Primeval: of or relating to the earliest ages.

The ancient chaos.

Thoth is saying, "So, I can have a glimpse of the ancient times." He's talking about seeing back to a primitive era, like looking at a small tract of land in North America that still has remnants of primeval forest. We're talking about taking a peek back in time. Through this portal, he's able to see a glimpse of the ancient times at the beginning, when everything was in chaos. That's what he's referring to.

> "Shuddered my soul to the vision of horror, shrank back my soul from the ocean of darkness. Then saw I the need for the barriers,"

Portal Barrier Representation

As you can see, beyond these mansions, barriers, and gates that keep this holographic dimension in place, there's a portal. This portal opens to an area that, if it weren't gated and blocked, could actually intersect and interfere with where we are right now. That's why these barriers are there.

It was horrifying. And this guy has seen everything you can imagine, and this horrified him to the point where he shrank back; the experience shrank back his soul. He jumped back, like, "Whoa" from the ocean of darkness.

> "Then saw I the need for the barriers, saw the need for the Lords of Arulu."

These Lords are the ones who guard these gates. There's a real and true need for these guards.

Remember the Marvel movie "Thor" from 2011? Idris Elba played Heimdall, the guardian of the gates of Arulu. He stood watch day and night because beyond those gates lay primeval chaos, which persists even now. This chaos and the entities within it could, if they had the chance, access our realm consistently and destroy everything we know.

That's what those Marvel movies are really about—this primeval darkness and entities coming through a portal, trying to destroy Earth and everything else in the universe. In the movie, Heimdall gets attacked by one of these beings, and with him is Thor's brother, Loki. At some point, Heimdall is overpowered, allowing evil to come in and wreak havoc on his world.

Movies are "edu-tainment" if you really pay attention. If you know what these ancient texts and tablets say, and then you watch a movie, you'll be surprised to see that the writers got all their inspiration from these ancient tablets.

> "Shuddered my soul to the vision of horror, shrank back my soul from the ocean of darkness. Then saw I the need for the barriers, saw the need for the Lords of Arulu. Only they with their Infinite balance could stand in the way of the inpouring chaos. Only they could guard God's creation."

Now, let me make my case for the fractal holographic matrix again: The Duat, with its seven houses, serves as gateways to the twelve dimensions that hold this holographic matrix together. These gateways are protected from outside sources–by actual guards, making it all very real.

Thoth says,

> "Only they could guard God's creation."

He is acknowledging that this universe encapsulated in this holographic matrix, was created by God. This illusion with this Duat access and this illusionary multiple dimension was created by God.

> "Then did I pass 'round the circle of eight. Saw all the souls who had conquered the darkness. Saw the splendor of Light where they dwelled. Longed I to take my place in their circle, but longed I also for the way I had chosen, when I stood in the Halls of Amenti and made my choice to the work I would do."

In other words, Thoth wanted to stay in Arulu and dwell with the big rulers and the big leaders of the past who are there. He could have if he wanted to, but he remembered, "My mission isn't complete yet. I'm still working on my mission inside of God's creation."

> "Passed I from the Halls of Arulu down to the earth space where my body lay."

This verse is talking about the fact that Arulu has a portal connection down to the Halls of Amenti.

Yes, you read it right, folks.

The halls of Arulu have a direct portal link to the Halls of Amenti!

Ten

Wisdom of the Halls of Amenti

The Halls of Amenti

THOTH'S BODIES—HE HAS MULTIPLE BODIES IN THESE rejuvenation chambers—these bodies are not stolen bodies. They are clone bodies that he himself created, and he transfers his consciousness from one body to the next as he sees fit. He's done it a hundred times ten, and each body has sat in the chamber for a hundred years each. When you add that up, it's ten thousand years. It's crazy numbers.

> "Passed I from the Halls of Arulu down to the earth space where my body lay. Arose I from the earth where I rested. Stood I before the Dweller. Gave my pledge to renounce my Great right until my work on Earth was completed, until the Age of darkness be past."

Thoth told the dweller who had already said, "I authorize you. You can go dwell in the sphere of Arulu with all the people that have committed, that have done their work, completed their missions."

It was a test. It actually was a full-on test. And he passed that test because he told the dweller that, "I renounce my great right. I'm not going to Arulu yet, until my work on earth is completed; until the age of darkness be passed."

So, what was he talking about?

He is saying that he's not done working on earth until the golden age arrives.

Where's Thoth Now? Where Has He Gone? What is He Doing?

He's still here. And guess what? The mission is not complete. And he will remain here until this mission is complete.

The mission is to see mankind regain its birthright in a golden age.

Once we reclaim a new golden age, he will then claim his birthright from all the work that he has done, and he will dwell in Arulu. But right now, Thoth is here.

> "Gave my pledge to renounce my Great right until my work on Earth was completed, until the Age of darkness be past. List ye, o man, to the words I shall give ye. In them shall ye find the Essence of Life. Before I return to the Halls of Amenti, taught shall ye be the Secrets of Secrets, how ye, too, may arise to the Light."

We'll be taught on how we ourselves can rise to this same light.

> "Preserve them and guard them, hide them in symbols, so the profane will laugh and renounce. In every land, form ye the mysteries. Make the way hard for the seeker to tread."

So, let's read this again.

> "I return to the Halls of Amenti, taught shall ye be."

He's saying, "When I return to the Halls of Amenti, you guys and girls will be taught. You will be learned people. The initiates will have the knowledge."

He has no fear in that. It will be done. You'll have the secret of secrets on how we too can arise to the light. How we can become like him, how we can rise to the light; from darkness to light.

> "Preserve them and guard them."

Preserve these secrets and guard these secrets. He says, hide them in symbols, so the profane will laugh and renounce.

You know what the symbols are nowadays that the profane laugh at?

Those are the memes that we post. While they're posting pictures of their cat and pictures of what they ate for dinner last night, and photos of street fights and people getting murdered in the streets, and women half naked, we're posting memes about consciousness. We are posting memes about ancient wisdom and true ancient history.

And they're laughing at us, trolling us, and commenting negatively about us, but guess what?

We're hiding them in symbols. Only the adept can see the esoteric wisdom, only they can discern it and gain knowledge. For the profane, it goes in one ear and out the other, bouncing off their eyes as if the photon never got absorbed by their brain. The profane will laugh and renounce it.

In Every Land, Form Ye the Mysteries

What's the number one watched show on 4bidden Knowledge TV? The Egyptian Mystery School. That's the number one watched series. Thirty-nine episodes of Egyptian Mysteries taught by me on 4bidden Knowledge TV. If you don't have a subscription to my TV network and you want to watch that, you see, I've obeyed the commandments.

Egyptian Mystery School

The commandment is to form the mysteries, which is exactly what I've done.

It says,

> "Make the way hard for the seeker to tread."

These profane people, they're not even going to think about subscribing. You just can't roll everything out on YouTube. For seekers, I put out more information than probably anyone else in the social media community. With my team, we have about one hundred forty accounts and probably post thirty to forty times per day across all platforms. That's a lot of information. But to access the higher levels of knowledge and the more secret information, you've got to pay for workshops and sign up for 4bidden Knowledge TV. That makes it challenging for the true seeker to tread this path.

> "Thus will the weak and the wavering be rejected. Thus will the secrets be hidden and guarded, held till the time when the wheel shall be turned. Through the dark ages, waiting and watching, my Spirit shall remain in the deep hidden land. When one has passed all the trials of the outer, summon ye me by the Key that ye hold."

So, Thoth is letting us know that he can be summoned with a key, and he and the key ends up being in our hands.

Let me make sure you guys are on the same page as me.

Thoth says,

> "Then will I, the Initiator, answer, come from the Halls of the Gods in Amenti. Then will I receive the initiate, give him the words of power."

He will leave his rejuvenation chamber at this point.

> "Then will I receive the initiate, give him the words of power. Hark ye, remember, these words of warning: bring not to me one lacking in wisdom, impure in heart or weak in his purpose. Else I will withdraw from ye your power to summon me from the place of my sleeping."

He's saying, don't waste my freaking time. When you call on me, things better be right. Don't make me wake up for no reason, or I will withdraw your power. I'll take your power away.

> "Go forth and conquer the element of darkness. Exalt in thy nature thine essence of Light. Now go ye forth and summon thy brothers so that I may impart the wisdom to light thy path when my presence is gone."

You see what the verse says there?

> "Now go ye forth and summon thy brothers."

That's what we're doing now. That's what you're doing as you read this book. I've summoned you to be here, in this present moment, reading these words. And here you are, gaining the light and information from Thoth directly at this moment.

At the time that he decides to leave or is gone working on something else, somewhere else, we have the knowledge and wisdom to continue on.

> "Come to the chamber beneath my temple. Eat not food until three days are past."

Thoth is talking about fasting. Coming into the chamber and he's talking about fasting for three days.

> "There will I give thee the essence of wisdom so that with power ye may shine amongst men. There will I give unto thee the secrets so that ye, to, may rise to the Heavens—God-men in Truth as in essence ye be."

Thoth is telling you that when you come sit with him, you'll fast for three days. That doesn't mean that you're sitting physically in front of him. You are doing this purposefully, using the knowledge and insight you already possess. He is telling you that you will fast for three days, take this knowledge, and take the fact that you have honored this knowledge so that you are not wasting his time. And you will summon him.

The benefit of this is,

> "There will I give unto thee the secrets so that ye, to, may rise to the Heavens—God-men in Truth as in essence ye be."

Thoth also says,

> "Depart now and leave me while I summon those ye know of but as yet know not."

Now, that's deep.

He's saying, "I've taught you. Go and leave my presence, because I am going to summon people that you do not even know yet." These are the people you will interact with because he needs them on this path as well, as they are pieces to this puzzle. They may be navigating in darkness at this moment, but he's going to nudge them in our direction and then when we get ahold of them, we have to bring them to the light through trials and testing and through revealing secreted knowledge.

Navigating the Darkness

Powerful stuff. Wow! Truly deep.

So much of this alluded me in the first few years, which is why I didn't really break them down in *Compendium of the Emerald Tablets*.

Eleven
Emerald Tablet 15

Now, we're going to examine Tablet 15 in detail. We need to complete our discussion and move into the topic of frequencies, which I know many of you have been eagerly waiting for.

> "Now ye assemble, my children, waiting to hear the Secret of Secrets."

This message has been talked about in the previous tablets many times, alluding to this "Secret of secrets." We're finally going to get to the Secret of Secrets in this tablet.

> "Now ye assemble, my children, waiting to hear the Secret of Secrets which shall give ye power to unfold the God-man, give ye the way to Eternal life."

In other words, the Godman already exists in you, but it must be "unfolded" for you to tap into it. Once you tap into the power that's truly in you, you now become the God-man.

> ". . . give ye the way to Eternal life. Plainly shall I speak of the Unveiled Mysteries. No dark sayings shall I give unto thee. Open thine ears now, my children. Hear and obey the words that I give."

What Thoth means to say is that he is going to give this to you straight up, no chaser. You're getting ready to get the raw information. "Pay attention," is what he's saying.

> "First I shall speak of the fetters of darkness which bind ye in chains to the sphere of the Earth."

Thoth reminds us that the reason we are stuck on this prison planet, trapped in the reincarnation cycle, is because of these fetters—these things that hold us down. We keep trying to carry all these emotional and physical burdens with us, believing we can hold onto them lifetime after lifetime without releasing them. He is saying that these fetters are what keep resetting this video game for us, making us start from the beginning over and over again. That's why we keep coming back here.

It's the fetters that bind.

> "Darkness and light are both of one nature, different only in seeming, for each arose from the source of all."

What did God say in the Bible?

He said in Isaiah,

> "I create the darkness and I create the light. Do what I sayeth the Lord."

Thoth says darkness and light are both in one nature, different only in seeming. It's the same thing in the Bible.

Do you see where a lot of the biblical text is coming from?

> "Darkness and light are both of one nature, different only in seeming, for each arose from the source of all. Darkness is disorder. Light is Order. Darkness transmuted is light of the Light. This, my children, your purpose in being; transmutation of darkness to light."

Some of you may have heard me say this before. Right now, I'm sitting in a well-lit room. There is no amount of darkness that I can inject into this room that would make it dark in here. The only way to make this room dark would be to turn the light off.

But I can't inject darkness into this room to make it dark!

However, if I turn all the lights off and make it completely dark in here, all I would need to do is turn on the flashlight from my cell phone camera.

Darkness Flees from Light

And guess what?

The darkness would flee instantly from that tiny light! The smallest amount of light will make darkness flee!

But there's no amount of darkness that can make light flee.

Do you see?

This is why it's important for us to become the light! This is why that term and that phrase has been said so many dozens of times, throughout these tablets.

> "Hear ye now of the mystery of nature, the relations of life to the Earth where it dwells. Know ye, ye are threefold in nature, physical, astral and mental in one."

In nature, man is threefold. We're a physical being, we have astral body, which is our spirit body, and we have a mental nature as well. These are three individual characteristics that make up a man.

> "Three are the qualities of each of the natures; nine in all, as above, so below."

Thoth is saying it isn't just humans, it's also the people on higher planes of existence, have the same setup, the same makeup.

Isn't that interesting?

That's huge because it's telling you that no matter where you look, you're going to see this same exact setup.

As above, so below–Physical, astral, and mental.

The Idea of Physical, Astral & Mental Body

"In the physical are these channels, the blood which moves in vortical motion, reacting on the heart to continue its beating. Magnetism which moves through the nerve paths, carrier of energies to all cells and tissues. Akasa which flows through channels, subtle yet physical, completing the channels. Each of the three attuned with each other, each affecting the life of the body. Form they the skeletal framework through which the subtle ether flows. In their mastery lies the Secret of Life in the body. Relinquished only by will of the adept, when his purpose in living is done."

He's talking about Qigong now.

> "In their mastery lies the Secret of Life in the body. Relinquished only by will of the adept,"

Okay, let me go back a little bit here.

> "In the physical are these channels, the blood which moves in vortical motion, reacting on the heart to continue its beating."

He says that now, magnetism is what's moving through the nerve paths. We know from modern science that electromagnetism, the electrical charge in the body, causes movement up and down the nerve paths, serving as the carrier of energy to the cells and tissues.

That's crazy because this is ancient wisdom.

> "Akasa which flows through channels, subtle yet physical, completing the channels."

Now, here's where it gets really powerful.

> "Each of the three attuned with each other, each affecting the life of the body. Form they the skeletal framework through which the subtle ether flows."

This is talking about the Qigong energy, the movement of Qi through the body.

> "In their mastery," when you master these energies, "lies the Secret of Life in the body. Relinquished only by will of the adept, when his purpose in living is done."

In other words, you can control when you leave this physical body once you master these aspects. When you master the nature of man, you gain the power to incarnate at will. You have the power to leave this body when you feel your purpose for living is done.

If you remember, Thoth renounced his right to live in Arulu because he said his work on Earth wasn't complete. So, he came back through the gate, entered through the Duat, returned to Earth, went to the Halls of Amenti, got himself a new body, and went back to work again.

We have the same power!

> "Three are the natures of the Astral, mediator is between above and below; not of the physical, not of the Spiritual, but able to move above and below. Three are the natures of Mind, carrier it of the Will of the Great One. Arbitrator of Cause and Effect in thy life. Thus is formed the threefold being, directed from above by the power of four. Above and beyond man's threefold nature lies the realm of the Spiritual Self. Four is it in qualities, shining in each of the planes of existence, but thirteen in one, the mystical number. Based on the qualities of man are the Brothers: each shall direct the unfoldment of being, each shall channels be of the Great One."

Now, let's break this down. He says,

> "Three are the natures of the Astral, mediator is between above and below; not of the physical, not of the Spiritual, but able to move above and below."

He's talking about the astral body having the capability to leave your physical body and project itself and move through this dimension or even into higher dimensions.

MYSTERIES OF THE FORBIDDEN EMERALD TABLETS

The astral body leaving the physical body

Thoth is saying that there is the nature of the mind, and the Great One–the carrier of will.

The first Hermetic principle written by Thoth the Atlantean is,

"All is mind."

What this means is that the nature of the mind is the carrier of will. In other words, You have the power to will things into existence. You have the power to form a command and create your future realities.

Twelve
Universal Balance

"Arbitrator of Cause and Effect in thy life."

ONCE YOU MAKE A CONSCIOUS DECISION THROUGH WILL, THERE will be a consequence.

Every decision you make and act on will create a consequence. It'll be a "good" consequence or a "bad" consequence. But I guarantee you, there will always be a consequence because it's an arbitrator of cause and effect.

The way to become wise at utilizing this understanding of knowledge that's already embedded and encoded into you, is anytime you must make a decision about anything, you consider several possible outcomes before making your choice.

- *If I do this, let me meditate on that. This is the potential outcome.*
- *If I do it this way, let me meditate on that. I can foresee now; this is the potential outcome.*
- *If I do it this way, this is the potential outcome.*

So, what you're doing is you're traveling through space and time. You're sending your mind outside of space and time and you're actually foreseeing future potential realities that could exist based on a decision that you make now.

Understand that you are the arbitrator of cause and effect, which means, you and I have the capability of sending out a ripple in space and time based on the activity, action, and decisions we make today. That ripple will go out and at some point in the future, we will cross-connect and intersect with that ripple; that will be the reality that we have created.

You can create that reality by understanding and taking the time, the space between decision and action, to meditate and foresee the outcome, so that the outcome that you desire is in your reality tunnel and not some random outcome that blindsides you.

> "Above and beyond man's threefold nature lies the realm of the Spiritual Self."

Your higher self.

Sending "energy" or light to the physical self

We are not here; we're picking up a frequency from a higher self, from a higher dimension. Our avatar body is encapsulating and holding it temporally over time, for a short period of time and before it's released again.

But Thoth has a key to release his entanglement from this corporeal body at will.

> "Four is it in qualities, shining in each of the planes of existence, but thirteen in one, the mystical number. Based on the qualities of man

are the Brothers: each shall direct the unfoldment of being, each shall channels be of the Great One."

We are all channels of the Great One.

When you turn on your TV or an old-fashioned radio, they receive signals from a single broadcasting station in your area. This station sends out multiple channels on radio waves, which are a form of light. Your receiver, whether it's a car radio, home radio, or TV with antennas, can pick up these signals.

Frequencies with Light

All these signals come from one source, but each device tunes to a different frequency.

It's the same with us.

One source is sending out multiple frequencies. For example, your body might be tuned to 99.1 FM, mine might be tuned to 99.2 FM, Jack's might be tuned to 99.3 FM, and Sue's might be tuned to 99.4 FM. This means we are all receiving from the same source signal, which is God, but we each receive it on a slightly different frequency that our physical bodies are tuned to receive.

There's a consistent and persistent stream of light being received by our avatars, giving us the illusion that we are separate individuals. But in reality, we are all connected to and coming from a higher source, and that higher source is transmitting to us all.

> "On Earth, man is in bondage, bound by space and time to the earth plane. Encircling each planet, a wave of vibration, binds him to his plane of unfoldment. Yet within man is the Key to releasement, within man may freedom be found."

The key to being free is already inside us. That's why I always say, go to inner space. You must embark on a journey to inner space.

Forget about outer space. The key to the answers to all your problems and to unlocking who you truly are is already inside you.

Now, we're getting into frequencies.

> "When ye have released the self from the body, rise to the outermost bounds of your earth-plane. Speak ye the word Dor-E-Lil-La."

Pronunciation: Dor-E-Lil-La

So, what's happening here?

Thoth is talking about when you're free. This is not something you say to get free; this is something that you say once you are free.

But he's saying that once you're actually free from this physical corporeal body, when you get to the bound, which is the edge of the earth boundary,

> "Speak ye the word Dor-E-Lil-La."

That's a frequency, it's a code.

What is it a code to?

It's a code to the gate. It's a code to get into and get through the gate in your spirit body.

Notice something interesting here, that even in your spirit body, you have the ability to speak. Even in the spirit body, in your light body, you still have the ability to speak.

Isn't that interesting?

> "Then for a time your Light will be lifted, free may ye pass the barriers of space. For a time of half of the sun,"

—six hours is what he's talking about here. I figured it all out.

> "Then for a time your Light will be lifted, free may ye pass the barriers of space. For a time of half of the sun (six hours), free may ye pass the barriers of earth-plane, see and know those who are beyond thee."

He's talking about for six hours, you'll have the ability to explore, but you're only going to get six hours.

> "Yea, to the highest worlds may ye pass. See your own possible heights of unfoldment, know all earthly futures of Soul. Bound are ye in your body, but by the power ye may be free. This is the Secret whereby bondage shall be replaced by freedom for thee."

You'll be able to even look into the future and see your own future because you're in a higher dimension. You can see the past, present, and future all at once.

Depiction of seeing the future

Next, Thoth speaks of the technique to be used to achieve this feat:

"Calm let thy mind be."

It says calm your mind, in other words, reduce your thoughts.

"At rest, be thy body:"

Get comfortable. Get into a comfortable position. It doesn't have to be the lotus position. Just get into a very comfortable position. Preferably, I would think maybe even lying on your back.

Man Resting in a Comfortable Position

"At rest be thy body: Conscious only of freedom from flesh."

YOU'RE ONLY FOCUSING on the spirit body being free from this physical body. That is your main focus.

> "Center thy being on the goal of thy longing. Think over and over that thou wouldst be free. Think of this word—La-Um-I-L-Gan—over and over in thy mind let it sound. Drift with the sound to the place of thy longing. Free from the bondage of flesh by thy will."

You're going to be speaking that word in your mind. That is not somebody's name. That's an actual frequency.

So, you're lying on your back, your body is fully relaxed, you're focusing on leaving your body, maybe even focusing on where you want to send your astral body to, and you're going to begin to say,

"La-Um-I-L-Gan"

Pronunciation: La-Um-I-L-Gan

over and over.

> "... in thy mind let it sound. Drift with the sound to the place of thy longing."

As you repeat this word, focus on the thought that you are actually moving to the place you want to be. Wherever that is for you, it will be different for everyone.

> "Free from the bondage of flesh by thy will."

This is how you can initiate an astral projection. You can leave your physical body and go on a little trip for about six hours, using this technique.

ENTERING the Halls of Amenti

Mysteries of the Forbidden Emerald Tablets

"Hear ye while I give the greatest of secrets: how ye may enter the Halls of Amenti, enter the place of the immortals as I did, stand before the Lords in their places."

This is powerful stuff!

If you ever go to Egypt with me, I'll take you to Enki's Halls of Amenti, where the rejuvenation chambers of the dwellers are located. I'll even show you how to climb up and get inside one of these chambers.

My trip to the Halls of Amenti

"Hear ye while I give the greatest of secrets: how ye may enter the Halls of Amenti, enter the place of the immortals as I did, stand before the Lords in their places. Lie ye down in rest of thy body. Calm thy mind so no thought disturbs thee. Pure must ye be in mind and in purpose, else only failure will come unto thee."

Thoth is talking about how you can enter the Halls of Amenti. Here's the technique: lay down, rest your body, calm your mind, quiet your thoughts. Be pure in mind and purpose; nothing deceptive, nothing dark.

If your heart and your mind are pure, you may be able to pass.

"Vision Amenti as I have told in my Tablets. Long with fullness of heart to be there. Stand before the Lords in thy mind's eye."

In your mind's eye, envision yourself in Amenti standing before the seven Lords.

"Pronounce the words of power I give (mentally); *Mekut-EI-Shab-El Hale-Sur-Ben-EI-Zabrut Zin-Efrim-Quar-EI.*"

Pronunciation: Mekut-EI-Shab-El Hale-Sur-Ben-EI-Zabrut Zin-Efrim-Quar-EI

SAY these words mentally and you're going to do that over and over again. These are frequencies.

This is a cymatics frequency.

"Mekut-EI-Shab-El Hale-Sur-Ben-EI-Zabrut Zin-Efrim-Quar-EI."

Silently repeat this over and over again while relaxing your body, being of pure heart and pure of mind, envisioning the Halls of Amenti, envisioning yourself standing there before the seven Lords.

At some point in that meditation, you will enter the Halls of Amenti.

> "Now give I the Key to Shamballa, the place where my Brothers live in the darkness: Darkness but filled with Light of the Sun—Darkness of Earth, but Light of the Spirit, guides for ye when my day is done."

So, you will be given the key to Shamballa, an incredible, magical place, a Heaven-like paradise mentioned in books all over the world. Ironically, the same name, Shamballa, appears in various writings from different parts of the world. Once you can achieve entering the Halls of Amenti through the technique above, you'll be given the keys to Shamballa.

> "Leave thou thy body as I have taught thee. Pass to the barriers of the deep, hidden place. Stand before the gates and their guardians. Command thy entrance by these words: "I am the Light. In me is no darkness. Free am I of the bondage of night. Open thou the way of the Twelve and the One, so I may pass to the realm of wisdom."

Once you have received the key to Shamballa, you do another astral projection using the same technique. But now, when you reach to these gates, after passing through Duat, you will have to enter the gate, where you will see guardians.

You're going to command them.

This is the key phrase:

> "I am the Light. In me is no darkness. Free am I of the bondage of

night. Open thou the way of the Twelve and the One, so I may pass to the realm of wisdom."

This is the secret to get past the guards and through the gate.

"When they refuse thee, as surely they will, command them to open by these words of power:"

Now, we're getting into the frequency you must give them.

"I am the Light. For me are no barriers. Open, I command, by the Secret of Secrets—Edom-EI-Ahim-Sabbert-Zur Adorn."

Now, Edom-El-Ahim is interesting because we know that Edom is mentioned in the Bible, specifically in the Torah. The name Elohim, which is sometimes written as El-Ahim, is the ancient term used to refer to gods in the plural form.

Sabbert-Zur Adorn is essentially stating, "I am a God-man, a Man of Light, and I command that these gates be opened." This declaration underscores your identity and authority as a divine being.

But this is a frequency.

Edom-EI-Ahim-Sabbert-Zur Adorn.

Pronunciation: Edom-EI-Ahim-Sabbert-Zur Adorn

And when you say this, they have to open the gates. They have to let you in. The guard must allow you access.

These frequencies have the power to open the gate.

The guards of the gate in some way, have the ability to take this frequency and access the gate and open it up for you.

> "Then if thy words have been "Truth" of the highest, open for thee the barriers will fall. Now, I leave thee, my children. Down, yet up, to the Halls shall I go."

He's going down to the Halls of Amenti, but he is actually ascending upward into higher dimensions, while his body is rejuvenating in the rejuvenation chambers.

> "Win ye the way to me, my children. Truly my brothers shall ye become."

That's interesting because in John 14:2, Jesus says,

> "In my father's house, there are many mansions. If it were not so, I would've told you, I go to prepare a place for you. And if I go and prepare a place for you, I will come again and receive you unto myself. That where I am, there, ye may be also."

It's the same meaning said in different ways.

> "Win ye the way to me, my children. Truly my brothers shall ye become."

I'm telling you that Yeshua is the same person as Thoth.

> "Thus finish I my writings. Keys let them be to those who come after. But only to those who seek my wisdom, for only for these am I the Key and the Way."

Interesting, isn't it?

Read it slowly so you can hear it; it's a very powerful statement.

In John 14, Jesus says unto them,

> "I am the truth, the way and the life. No man cometh unto the Father, but by me. I am the key and the way."

Jesus says,

> "I am the way."

Interesting. Very interesting indeed!

Let's go over some of these frequencies.

> "By their names I call them to aid me, free me and save me from the darkness of night: Untanas, Quertas, Chietal, and Goyana, Huer-tal,

Semveta—Ardal. By their names I implore thee, free me from darkness and fill me with Light."

In this verse, Thoth explains that the names mentioned in the Emerald Tablets are not just names of people but are actually frequencies. These frequencies are representative of certain vibrational energies and states of being. In my book, *Compendium of the Emerald Tablets*, I talk about the meanings behind these frequencies and their significance in the context of the teachings of Thoth.

There are times when you're in a situation that requires prayer. When people are trying to pray, they're trying to cast a spell.

Wait, praying is casting a spell?

People may not want to admit it, but that's often why they pray. Whether something has gone wrong or something has gone right and they want to acknowledge it, most of the time, they're trying to change a situation they don't like or fix a problem.

So, people pray. But here's the thing—prayer often doesn't work for them because they don't really know how to pray. And that's just a fact.

Thoth instructs us to find a dark, quiet space—like a room or a closet—where we can stand up straight with our hands in the air. Envision a circle around you, and then utter the sacred names.

Untanas, Quertas, Chietal, and Goyana, Huer-tal, Semveta—Ardal

Pronunciation: Untanas, Quertas, Chietal, and Goyana, Huer-tal, Semveta—Ardal

By uttering these words with the right frequency—Untanas, Quertas, Chietal, Goyana, Huer-tal, Semveta, Ardal—you can change your reality. While focusing on the change you want, speak these words aloud. The vibrations of these words will empower you to alter your reality. You can repeat this process for different situations or even just to calm yourself down.

It's important to remember that these frequencies have power over space and time. They have power over reality, which is why Thoth taught these. So, if you're going to pray and cast a spell, you might as well do it the right way.

By focusing on the outcome that you specifically want, and uttering these frequencies—these names of these frequencies–these tones through your own vocal box will help to alter the future reality, your future reality in the third dimension.

Also, we look at the long one here underneath Dor-E-Lil-La. Let's go underneath that.

Mekut-EI-Shab-El Hale-Sur-Ben-EI-Zabrut Zin-Efrim-Quar-EI

Say these when you're focusing on your astral projection, when you're leaving the physical body. This is your astral projection. Make sure you're lying down in a quiet place, and your mind is calm.

If you can't calm your mind, envision a bowl in your mind. Now, visualize your thoughts in that bowl. See the bowl full of thoughts.

Now, envision a hand reaching into the bowl and removing some of the thoughts. Just imagine the hand picking them up and dropping them outside of the bowl, letting them go. Watch the hand repeat this process, over and over.

Even while I'm visualizing this right now, my thoughts are reducing significantly. My mind is now calm. It's that quick.

When you first start visualizing, it might take you a minute, two minutes, or even five minutes to get it right, but with practice it will become easier. I can do it now within less than a minute, and I can have my mind almost completely clear. Even while I was writing, my thoughts were reducing.

Once you get your mind to calm down to a minimum level, the next step is to focus is on where you want to go as you begin to chant that phrase over and over again, and envision yourself there.

The next frequency we will talk about is Dor-E-Lil-La.

You can begin to chant Dor-E-Lil-La once you've actually gotten free from your body, risen to the outermost bounds of the earth plane, and you're ready to go through a gate to the higher worlds.

All these words are frequencies; they are actual cymatics that you're speaking. When you speak these words, you're engaging with specific sound vibrations that have power over gates, time, frequencies, and energy. You must understand that these cymatics, these sound patterns, have a profound impact on the world around us and on our own consciousness.

That's how powerful they are. Extra, extra super powerful stuff!

I hope you get a chance to practice. I've used these techniques already, and I've had extreme success, and so, I'm hoping you get a chance to experience some of what I've experienced.

Some of the magic happens when you truly focus and become adept, allowing yourself to free your mind from this physical body. As you become aware that we are in a matrix, you'll find the experience isn't surprising because you've known it exists. However, going through it is still a profound experience.

Thirteen
Step by Step Instructions

Step One: Clear Your Mind

Before I provide the instructions from the Emerald Tablets, I want to remind you of the technique for clearing your mind, which can be helpful for the following exercises. Here are the steps I use to clear my mind:

Meditation Bowl

1. Envision a bowl in your mind.
2. Visualize your thoughts filling that bowl.
3. See the bowl full of thoughts.
4. Imagine a hand reaching into the bowl.
5. Picture the hand picking up several thoughts and dropping them outside of the bowl, letting them go.
6. Watch the hand repeat this process over and over.

When you first start visualizing, it might take a minute, two minutes, or even five minutes to get it right. But don't worry, it will become easier with practice. Keep practicing until you feel comfortable with it. Once you're confident that you can calm your mind, you can move on to the instructions given in the Emerald Tablets.

Step Two: Releasing Darkness

The Text

> "Given to man have they secrets that shall guard and protect him from all harm. He who would travel the path of a master, free must he be from the bondage of night. Conquer must he the formless and shapeless; conquer must he the phantom of fear. Knowing, must he gain of all the secrets, travel the pathway that leads through the darkness, yet ever before him keep the light of his goal. Obstacles great shall he meet in the pathway, yet press on to the Light of the Sun.

Mysteries of the Forbidden Emerald Tablets

Light of the Sun in Space

Hear ye, O man, the Sun is the symbol of the Light that shines at the end of thy road. Now to thee give I the secrets: how to meet the dark power, meet and conquer the fear from the night. Only by knowing can ye conquer; only by knowing can ye have Light.

Now I give unto thee the knowledge, known to the Masters; the knowing that conquers all the dark fears. Use this, the wisdom I give thee. Master thou shalt be of the Brothers of Night.

When unto thee there comes a feeling, drawing thee nearer to the dark gate, examine thine heart and find if the feeling thou hast has come from within. If thou shalt find the darkness thine own thoughts, banish them forth from place in thy mind. Send through thy body a wave of vibration, irregular first and regular second, repeating time after time until free. Start the Wave Force in thy Brain Center. Direct it in waves from thine head to thy foot.

But if thou findest thine heart is not darkened, be sure that a force is directed to thee. Only by knowing can thou overcome it. Only by wisdom can thou hope to be free.

Knowledge brings wisdom and wisdom is power. Attain and ye shall have power o'er all.

Seek ye first a place bound with darkness. Place ye a circle around about thee. Stand erect in the midst of the circle. Use thou this formula, and thou shalt be free. Raise thou thine hands to the dark space above thee. Close thou thine eyes and draw in the Light. Call to the Spirit of Light through the Space- Time, using these words and thou shalt be free

"Fill thou my body with Spirit of Light. Come from the Flower that shines through the darkness. Come from the Halls where the Seven Lords rule. Name them by name, I, the Seven: Three, Four, Five and Six, Seven, Eight— Nine. By their names I call them to aid me, free me and save me from the darkness of night: Untanas, Quertas, Chietal, and Goyana, Huertal, Semveta—Ardal. By their names I implore thee, free me from darkness and fill me with Light."

Know ye, O man, that when ye have done this, ye shall be free from the fetters that bind ye, cast off the bondage of the Brothers of Night. See ye not that the names have the power to free by vibration the fetters that bind? Use them at need to free thou thine brother so the he, too, may come forth from the night.

Thou, O man, art thy brother's helper. Let him not lie in the bondage of night. Now unto thee, give I my magic. Take it and dwell on the pathway of Light. Light unto thee, Life unto thee, Sun may thou be on the cycle above."

THE INSTRUCTIONS

This is a two-part process.

Part One

1. When you feel any "darkness" or negativity, examine your heart and determine if the negative thought, feeling, or emotion comes from within you. (be honest)
2. If you find darkness in your thoughts, banish them from your mind.
3. Send a wave of vibration through your body, irregular first and regular second,
4. Start the Wave Force in your Brain Center.
5. Direct it in waves from your head to your foot.
6. Repeat this process until you are free from dark or negative thoughts and feelings.

Part Two

1. Find a dark, quiet space. (like a dark room or a closet)
2. Place a circle around yourself. (You can envision a circle.)
3. Stand up straight in the middle of the circle.
4. Raise your hands into the darkness above you.
5. Close your eyes
6. Draw in the Light.
7. Call to the Spirits of Light thro the Space-Time by saying:

"Fill thou my body with Spirit of Light. Come from the Flower that shines through the darkness. Come from the Halls where the Seven Lords rule. Name them by name, I, the Seven: Three, Four, Five and Six, Seven, Eight— Nine. By their names I call them to aid me, free me and save me from the darkness of night: Untanas, Quertas, Chietal, and Goyana, Huertal, Semveta—Ardal. By their names I implore thee, free me from darkness and fill me with Light."

1. Speak and repeat the sacred names out loud: *Untanas, Quertas, Chietal, and Goyana, Huer-tal, Semveta—Ardal*
2. Focus on the change you want

Pronunciation:: Untanas, Quertas, Chietal, and Goyana, Huer-tal, Semveta—Ardal

Remember, the vibrations of these words will empower you to alter your reality. You can repeat this process for different situations or even just to calm yourself down.

These frequencies have power over space and time. They have power over reality, which is why Thoth taught these. So, if you're going to pray and cast a spell, you might as well do it the right way.

By focusing on the outcome that you specifically want and uttering these frequencies—these names of these frequencies–these tones through your own vocal box will help to alter the future reality, your future reality in the third dimension.

Step Three: Astral Projection

The Text

Pronunciations of the Phrases needed for these exercises

"On Earth, man is in bondage, bound by space and time to the earth plane. Encircling each planet, a wave of vibration, binds him to his plane of unfoldment. Yet within man is the Key to releasement, within man may freedom be found.

When ye have released the self from the body, rise to the outermost bounds of your earth-plane. Speak ye the word Dor-E-Lil-La. Then for a time your Light will be lifted, free may ye pass the barriers of space. For a time of half of the sun (six hours), free may ye pass the barriers of earth- plane, see and know those who are beyond thee. Yea, to the highest worlds may ye pass. See your own possible heights of unfoldment, know all earthly futures of Soul.

Bound are ye in your body, but by the power ye may be free. This is the Secret whereby bondage shall be replaced by freedom for thee.

Calm let thy mind be. At rest be thy body: Conscious only of freedom from flesh. Center thy being on the goal of thy longing. Think over and over that thou wouldst be free. Think of this word—La-Um-I-L-Gan— over and over in thy mind let it sound. Drift with the sound to the place of thy longing. Free from the bondage of flesh by thy will."

The Instructions

This is a two-part process

Part One

1. Lay down and rest your body.
2. Calm your mind.
3. Center your thoughts on your goal of being free from your body.
4. Think over and over that you would be free
5. Think of this word over and over, letting your mind sound it out: *La-Um-I-L-Gan*
6. Drift with the sounds until you are free from the body.

Part Two

1. Once you have left your body, rise to the outermost bounds of the Earth Plane.
2. Speak the word: *Dor-E-Lil-La*
3. Chant this word if necessary.

4. Then you will have 6 hours to pass the barriers of space and into the highest worlds to see your highest possible unfoldment and know earthy futures of Soul.

Step Four: Entering the Halls of Amenti

The Text

"Hear ye while I give the greatest of secrets: how ye may enter the Halls of Amenti, enter the place of the immortals as I did, stand before the Lords in their places.

Lie ye down in rest of thy body. Calm thy mind so no thought disturbs thee. Pure must ye be in mind and in purpose, else only failure will come unto thee. Vision Amenti as I have told in my Tablets. Long with fullness of heart to be there. Stand before the Lords in thy mind's eye. Pronounce the words of power I give (mentally); Mekut-EI-Shab-El Hale-Sur-Ben-EI-Zabrut Zin-Efrim-Quar-EI. Relax thy mind and thy body. Then be sure your soul will be called."

The Instructions

1. Lay down and rest your body
2. Calm your mind and quiet your thoughts
3. Be pure in mind and purpose (nothing deceptive or dark)
4. In your mind's eye, envision yourself in Amenti, standing before the seven Lords
5. Repeatedly say these words in your mind:
   a. Mekut-EI-Shab-El Hale-Sur-Ben-EI-Zabrut Zin-Efrim-Quar-EI."

. . .

SILENTLY REPEAT this over and over again while relaxing your body, being of pure heart and pure of mind, envisioning the Halls of Amenti, envisioning yourself standing there before the seven Lords.

At some point in that meditation, you will enter the Halls of Amenti.

STEP FIVE: THE KEYS TO SHAMBALLA

Shamballa is an incredible, magical place, a Heaven-like paradise mentioned in books all over the world. Once you can achieve entering the Halls of Amenti through the technique above, you'll be given the keys to Shamballa.

To Shamballa

The Text

> "Now give I the Key to Shamballa, the place where my Brothers live in the darkness: Darkness but filled with Light of the Sun— Darkness of Earth, but Light of the Spirit, guides for ye when my day is done.

Leave thou thy body as I have taught thee. Pass to the barriers of the deep, hidden place. Stand before the gates and their guardians. Command thy entrance by these words: "I am the Light. In me is no darkness. Free am I of the bondage of night. Open thou the way of the Twelve and the One, so I may pass to the realm of wisdom." When they refuse thee, as surely they will, command them to open by these words of power: "I am the Light. For me are no barriers. Open, I command, by the Secret of Secrets— Edom-El-Ahim-Sabbert-Zur Adorn." Then if thy words have been "Truth" of the highest, open for thee the barriers will fall.

Now, I leave thee, my children. Down, yet up, to the Halls shall I go. Win ye the way to me, my children. Truly my brothers shall ye become.

Thus finish I my writings. Keys let them be to those who come after. But only to those who seek my wisdom, for only for these am I the Key and the Way."

The Instructions

Once you have received the key to Shamballa, you do another astral projection using the same technique. But now, when you reach to these gates, after passing through Duat, you will have to enter the gate, where you will see guardians.

1. Pass to the barriers of the deep, hidden place.
2. Stand before the gates and their guardians
3. Command your entrance using these words: "I am the Light. In me is no darkness. Free am I of the bondage of night. Open thou the way of the Twelve and the One, so I may pass to the realm of wisdom."
4. They will refuse you.

5. Then command, *"I am the Light. For me are no barriers. Open, I command, by the Secret of Secrets— Edom-EI-Ahim-Sabbert-Zur Adorn."*
6. This declaration underscores your identity and authority as a divine being. If you've spoken True of the highest, the barriers will fall and open for you.

Fourteen
Tablet 14 Complete Text

Becoming Thrice Great

List ye, O Man, to the deep hidden wisdom, lost to the world since the time of the Dwellers, lost and forgotten by men of this age.

Know ye this Earth is but a portal, guarded by powers unknown to man. Yet, the Dark Lords hide the entrance that leads to the Heaven-born land. Know ye, the way to the sphere of Arulu is guarded by barriers opened only to Light-born man.

Upon Earth, I am the holder of the keys to the gates of the Sacred Land. Command I, by the powers beyond me, to leave the keys to the world of man. Before I depart, I give ye the Secrets of how ye may rise from the bondage of darkness, cast off the fetters of flesh that have bound ye, rise from the darkness into the Light. Know ye, the soul must be cleansed of its darkness, ere ye may enter the portals of Light. Thus, I established among ye the Mysteries so that the Secrets may always be found. Aye, though man may fall into darkness, always the Light will shine as a guide. Hidden in darkness, veiled in symbols, always the way to the portal will be found. Man in the future will deny the mysteries but always the way the seeker will find.

religion

Regions there are two between this life and the Great One, traveled by the Souls who depart from this Earth; Duat, the home of the powers of illusion; Sekhet Hetspet, the House of the Gods. Osiris, the symbol of the guard of the portal, who turns back the souls of unworthy men. Beyond lies the sphere of the heaven-born powers, Arulu, the land where the Great Ones have passed. There, when my work among men has been finished, will I join the Great Ones of my Ancient home.

Seven are the mansions of the house of the Mighty; Three guards the portal of each house from the darkness; Fifteen the ways that lead to Duat. Twelve are the houses of the Lords of Illusion, facing four ways, each of them different. Forty and Two are the great powers, judging the Dead who seek for the portal. Four are the Sons of Horus, Two are the Guards of East and West— I sis, the mother who pleads for her children, Queen of the moon, reflecting the Sun. Ba is the essence, living forever. Ka is the Shadow that man knows as life. Ba cometh not until Ka is incarnate. These are mysteries to preserve through the ages. Keys are they of life and of Death. Hear ye now the mystery of mysteries: learn of the circle beginningless and endless, the form of He who is One and in all. Listen and hear it, go forth and apply it, thus will ye travel the way that I go. Mystery in Mystery, yet clear to the Light-born, the Secret of all I now will reveal. I will declare a secret to the initiated, but let the door be wholly shut against the profane.

Three is the mystery, come from the great one. Hear, and Light on thee will dawn.

In the primeval, dwell three unities. Other than these, none can exist. These are the

equilibrium, source of creation:

one God, one Truth, one point of freedom.

Three come forth from the three of the balance: all life, all good, all power.

Three are the qualities of God in his Light-home: Infinite power, Infinite Wisdom, Infinite Love.

Three are the powers given to the Masters: To transmute evil, assist good, use discrimination.

Three are the things inevitable for God to perform: Manifest power, wisdom and love.

Three are the powers creating all things: Divine Love possessed of perfect knowledge, Divine Wisdom knowing all possible means, Divine Power possessed by the joint will of Divine Love and Wisdom.

Three are the circles (states) of existence: The circle of Light where dwells nothing but God, and only God can traverse it; the circle of Chaos where all things by nature arise from death; the Circle of awareness where all things spring from life.

All things animate are of three states of existence: chaos or death, liberty in humanity and felicity of Heaven.

Three necessities control all things: beginning in the Great Deep, the circle of chaos, plenitude in Heaven.

Three are the paths of the Soul: Man, Liberty, Light.

Three are the hindrances: lack of endeavor to obtain knowledge; non-attachment to god; attachment to evil. In man, the three are manifest. Three are the Kings of power within. Three are the chambers of the mysteries, found yet not found in the body of man.

Hear ye now of he who is liberated, freed from the bondage of life into Light. Knowing the source of all worlds shall be open. Aye, even the Gates of Arulu shall not be barred. Yet heed, O man, who wouldst enter heaven. If ye be not worthy, better it be to fall into the fire. Know ye the celestials pass through the pure flame. At every revolution of the heavens, they bathe in the fountains of Light.

List ye, o man, to this mystery: Long in the past before ye were man-born, I dwelled in Ancient Atlantis. There in the Temple, I drank of the Wisdom, poured as a fountain of Light from the Dweller. Give the key to ascend to the Presence of Light in the Great world. Stood I before the Holy One enthroned in the flower of fire. Veiled was he by the lightnings of darkness, else my Soul by the Glory have been shattered.

Forth from the feet of his Throne like the diamond, rolled forth four rivers of flame from his footstool, rolled through the channels of clouds to the Man-world. Filled was the hall with Spirits of Heaven. Wonder of wonders was the Starry palace. Above the sky, like a rainbow of Fire and Sunlight, were formed the spirits. Sang they the glories of the Holy One. Then from the midst of the Fire came a voice: "Behold the Glory of the first Cause." I beheld that Light, high above all darkness, reflected in my own being. I attained, as it were, to the God of all Gods, the Spirit-Sun, the Sovereign of the Sun spheres.

Again came the Voice: "There is one, even the First, who hath no beginning, who hath no end; who hath made all things, who govern all, who is good, who is just, who illumines, who sustains."

Then from the throne, there poured a great radiance, surrounding and lifting my soul by its power. Swiftly I moved through the spaces of Heaven, shown was I the mystery of mysteries, shown the Secret heart of the cosmos. Carried was I to the land of Arulu, stood before the Lords in their Houses. Opened they the Doorway so I might glimpse the primeval chaos. Shuddered my soul to the vision of horror, shrank back my soul from the ocean of darkness. Then saw I the need for the barriers, saw the need for the Lords of Arulu. Only they with their Infinite balance could stand in the way of the inpouring chaos. Only they could guard God's creation.

Then did I pass 'round the circle of eight. Saw all the souls who had conquered the darkness. Saw the splendor of Light where they dwelled.

Longed I to take my place in their circle, but longed I also for the way I had chosen, when I stood in the Halls of Amenti and made my choice to the work I would do.

Passed I from the Halls of Arulu down to the earth space where my body lay. Arose I from the earth where I rested. Stood I before the Dweller. Gave my pledge to renounce my Great right until my work on Earth was completed, until the Age of darkness be past.

List ye, o man, to the words I shall give ye. In them shall ye find the Essence of Life. Before I return to the Halls of Amenti, taught shall ye be the Secrets of Secrets, how ye, too, may arise to the Light. Preserve them and guard them, hide them in symbols, so the profane will laugh and renounce. In every land, form ye the mysteries. Make the way hard for the seeker to tread. Thus will the weak and the wavering be rejected. Thus will the secrets be hidden and guarded, held till the time when the wheel shall be turned.

Through the dark ages, waiting and watching, my Spirit shall remain in the deep hidden land. When one has passed all the trials of the outer, summon ye me by the Key that ye hold. Then will I, the Initiator, answer, come from the Halls of the Gods in Amenti. Then will I receive the initiate, give him the words of power.

Hark ye, remember, these words of warning: bring not to me one lacking in wisdom, impure in heart or weak in his purpose. Else I will withdraw from ye your power to summon me from the place of my sleeping.

Go forth and conquer the element of darkness. Exalt in thy nature thine essence of Light.

Now go ye forth and summon thy brothers so that I may impart the wisdom to light thy path when my presence is gone. Come to the chamber beneath my temple. Eat not food until three days are past. There will I give thee the essence of wisdom so that with power ye may shine amongst men. There will I give unto thee the secrets so that ye, to , may rise to the Heavens— God- men in Truth as in essence ye be. Depart now and leave me while I summon those ye know of but as yet know not.

Fifteen
Tablet 15 Complete Text

Secret of Secrets

Now ye assemble, my children, waiting to hear the Secret of Secrets which shall give ye power to unfold the God-man, give ye the way to Eternal life. Plainly shall I speak of the Unveiled Mysteries. No dark sayings shall I give unto thee. Open thine ears now, my children. Hear and obey the words that I give.

First I shall speak of the fetters of darkness which bind ye in chains to the sphere of the Earth.

Darkness and light are both of one nature, different only in seeming, for each arose from the source of all. Darkness is disorder. Light is Order. Darkness transmuted is light of the Light. This, my children, your purpose in being; transmutation of darkness to light

Hear ye now of the mystery of nature, the relations of life to the Earth where it dwells. Know ye, ye are threefold in nature, physical, astral and mental in one. Three are the qualities of each of the natures; nine in all, as above, so below.

In the physical are these channels, the blood which moves in vortical motion, reacting on the heart to continue its beating. Magnetism which moves through the nerve paths, carrier of energies to all cells and tissues. Akasa which flows through channels, subtle yet physical, completing the channels. Each of the three attuned with each other, each affecting the life of the body. Form they the skeletal framework through which the subtle ether flows. In their mastery lies the Secret of Life in the body. Relinquished only by will of the adept, when his purpose in living is done.

Three are the natures of the Astral, mediator is between above and below; not of the physical, not of the Spiritual, but able to move above and below.

Three are the natures of Mind, carrier it of the Will of the Great One. Arbitrator of Cause and Effect in thy life. Thus is formed the threefold being, directed from above by the power of four. Above and beyond man's threefold nature lies the realm of the Spiritual Self. Four is it in qualities, shining in each of the planes of existence, but thirteen in one, the mystical number. Based on the qualities of man are the Brothers: each shall direct the unfoldment of being, each shall channels be of the Great One.

On Earth, man is in bondage, bound by space and time to the earth plane. Encircling each planet, a wave of vibration, binds him to his plane of unfoldment. Yet within man is the Key to releasement, within man may freedom be found.

When ye have released the self from the body, rise to the outermost bounds of your earth-plane. Speak ye the word Dor-E-Lil-La. Then for a time your Light will be lifted, free may ye pass the barriers of space. For a time of half of the sun (six hours), free may ye pass the barriers of earth- plane, see and know those who are beyond thee. Yea, to the highest worlds may ye pass. See your own possible heights of unfoldment, know all earthly futures of Soul.

Bound are ye in your body, but by the power ye may be free. This is the Secret whereby bondage shall be replaced by freedom for thee.

Calm let thy mind be. At rest be thy body: Conscious only of freedom from flesh. Center thy being on the goal of thy longing. Think over and over that thou wouldst be free. Think of this word— La-Um-I-L-Gan— over and over in thy mind let it sound. Drift with the sound to the place of thy longing. Free from the bondage of flesh by thy will.

Hear ye while I give the greatest of secrets: how ye may enter the Halls of Amenti, enter the place of the immortals as I did, stand before the Lords in their places.

Lie ye down in rest of thy body. Calm thy mind so no thought disturbs thee. Pure must ye be in mind and in purpose, else only failure will come unto thee. Vision Amenti as I have told in my Tablets. Long with fullness of heart to be there. Stand before the Lords in thy mind's eye. Pronounce the words of power I give (mentally); Mekut-EI-Shab- El Hale-Sur-Ben-EI-Zabrut Zin-Efrim-Quar-EI. Relax thy mind and thy body. Then be sure your soul will be called.

Now give I the Key to Shamballa, the place where my Brothers live in the darkness: Darkness but filled with Light of the Sun— Darkness of Earth, but Light of the Spirit, guides for ye when my day is done.

Leave thou thy body as I have taught thee. Pass to the barriers of the deep, hidden place. Stand before the gates and their guardians. Command thy entrance by these words: "I am the Light. In me is no darkness. Free am I of the bondage of night. Open thou the way of the Twelve and the One, so I may pass to the realm of wisdom." When they refuse thee, as surely they will, command them to open by these words of power: "I am the Light. For me are no barriers. Open, I command, by the Secret of Secrets— Edom-EI-Ahim-

Sabbert-Zur Adorn." Then if thy words have been "Truth" of the highest, open for thee the barriers will fall.

Now, I leave thee, my children. Down, yet up, to the Halls shall I go. Win ye the way to me, my children. Truly my brothers shall ye become.

Thus finish I my writings. Keys let them be to those who come after. But only to those who seek my wisdom, for only for these am I the Key and the Way.

Questions and Answers

When speaking with others about the topics I've presented in this book, there are some common questions that get asked about the Emerald Tablets. Whether you're looking for clarity, understanding or simply a different perspective, I will do my best to provide you with helpful answers.

Here we go:

Do you have to be on a high frequency to chant the words?

Well, we all want to stay on a high frequency, but let's be real—it's tough to maintain that all the time because we're human.

Typically, when you find yourself needing to chant those words and frequencies, it's because something has gone wrong and you need to make a change. When that happens, you're probably starting off at a lower frequency. But that's okay. The nature of being in a desperate situation means you'll start from a lower point and build your way up into a higher frequency as you gain confidence and control. So don't worry if you're not starting off high—just focus on getting there.

Have you tried the techniques you wrote about personally?

Yes, I did. And yes, I did travel!

Is there a recording of the phrases alone?

Use the QR code to access the audio files where I pronounce the phrases.

Pronunciation of Phrases

Have you ever heard of anyone, a person receiving their own personal passcodes?

I haven't heard of anyone that has received their own personal passcodes, but I do know people with the passcode.

How often do you practice leaving your body and using the frequency words? What has your experience been?

Well, I've practice it a few times. It's an amazing experience. I probably would've done a lot more, but I'm just very, very busy right now. It's just a lot to do, and it does take time.

But the experience is pretty amazing, because you begin to really, truthfully realize this is a matrix that we are living in. We are living in a fractal holographic matrix. It actually inspired me to write the book, ***Fractal Holographic Matrix by Billy Carson***. That's what inspired me.

Fractal Holographic Universe: The Matrix Code Revealed

Do you have any meditations that can help?

Yes! You can check it out on 4bidden Knowledge TV. Head to 4bk.tv or download the app from the iOS App Store for Apple devices, Google Play for Android devices, or get it on Apple TV, Roku, Amazon Fire TV, and Samsung TV. Just search for the 4bidden Knowledge TV app (with the number four) and watch the Egyptian

Mystery School series.

Did you experience a loud humming sound prior to your actual leaving the physical?

It wasn't a super loud humming sound, but I did experience a buzz. And when I left my physical body, I felt, I kind of heard this, "Pop." And the same thing happened on return as well.

What can be experienced by astral projection? What can I expect to see or learn from this?

What you're going to learn are two things. First, mastery over the physical form. Second, you'll experience the way this fractal holographic matrix looks and works from a completely different perspective. Once you enter the astral realm, you can see and experience this entire matrix in ways you can't in the physical form.

Is the whole point of this, all this work, is to gain wisdom of Thoth to regenerate like he could?

Part of it is to gain the wisdom needed to regenerate like Thoth. But the main goal is to help humanity find, seek, and become the light. We aim to be the lighthouse on the shoreline that others can see. Through our lives, by how we live and move, people should recognize us as a source of light and be drawn to us. This is the ultimate goal.

Does the pronunciation matter. Does adding our own way of saying it add power?

Well, the pronunciation does matter in some way. I'm pretty sure Thoth is aware that everyone has different accents on this planet, and pronouncing things in a specific, unified way, maybe extremely difficult for some people because of the accent. I'm pretty sure that the way I'm pronouncing these frequencies isn't exactly the way he would've pronounced it in the ancient times. So, I don't think, as long as they're being said, and enough of the vowels and the consonants are being annunciated, it should work.

Is it okay to open your eyes and read while meditating? Or should we memorize the frequencies first?

I think that it helps if you can memorize them. Initially, I think it would be okay to practice with your eyes open, until you learn them and memorize them. And then from there, do it with your eyes closed.

Woman Meditating

Thank you!

I want to sincerely thank each and every one of you, my readers, as we come to the close of the Mysteries of the Forbidden Emerald Tablets of Thoth.

This work would not exist without you. Thanks for investing your time in reading my book.

www.ingramcontent.com/pod-product-compliance
Lightning Source LLC
Chambersburg PA
CBHW071434160426
43195CB00013B/1895